C0-DUP-732

Timberdoodle

THIRD GRADE

Curriculum Handbook | 2024-2025

Nonreligious Edition

We're So Glad You Are Here

Congratulations on choosing to homeschool this year! Whether this is your first year as a teacher or your tenth, we're confident you'll find that there is very little that compares to watching your child's learning take off. We suspect you'll look back at this year as one that shaped your relationship with your child and made you closer than ever.

On Your Mark, Get Set, Go!

Preparing for your first school day is very easy. Peruse this guide, customize your schedule, browse the introductions in your books, and you will be ready to go.

We Are Here to Help

We would love to assist you if questions come up, so please don't hesitate to contact us with any questions, comments, or concerns. Whether you contact us by phone, email, or live online chat, you will get a real person who is eager to serve you and your family.

You Will Love This!

This year you and your student will learn more than you hoped while having a blast. Ready? Have an absolutely amazing year!

Schedule Customizer

Your 2024-2025 Third-Grade Nonreligious Curriculum Kit includes access to our Schedule Customizer, where you can not only plan out your school weeks but also tweak the checklist to include exactly what you want on your schedule. To get started, just visit the scheduling website:

schedule.timberdoodle.com

If you ordered online under the same email address as your Schedule Customizer account, your kit is preloaded and ready to schedule now! If not, use your activation code + order number to gain access now. (See page 12 for complete activation information.)

Your Timberdoodle Activation Code:

LUUENB6ENRAP

You'll also need your order number. If you ordered from a school district or don't have it handy, call, email, or chat with us, and we will be happy to look it up for you.

Get Support

Are you looking for a place to hang out online with like-minded homeschoolers? Do you wonder how someone else handled a particular science kit? Or do you wish you could encourage someone who is just getting started this year? Join one or more of our online groups.

Timberdoodlers of all ages:

https://www.facebook.com/groups/Timberdoodle

Timberdoodlers with 1st- to 4th-grade students:

https://www.facebook.com/groups/ElementaryTimberdoodle

Timberdoodlers using nonreligious kits:

https://www.facebook.com/groups/SecularTimberdoodle

Contents

Introductory
Matters

Meet Your Handbook

Simple Is Better

1. The Planning

First up are all the details on planning your year, including your annual planner and sample weekly checklists, which are the absolute backbones of Timberdoodle's curriculum kits. More on those in a moment.

2. Item-by-Item Introductions

We include short bios of each item in your kit, ideal for refreshing your memory on why each is included or explaining exactly what your student will be learning this year. This is where we've tucked in teaching tips to make this year easy and amazing for both of you.

3. Articles and Resources

In this section you'll find our favorite articles and tidbits gathered over 35 years of homeschool experience.

4. Item-Specific Resources

Here you'll find your 36-week schedule for Mosdos Opal.

5. Reading Challenge

Last but not least is the reading challenge—a reading log designed to help your child read a huge variety of books this year. We include hundreds of book ideas to give you a head start.

All the Details Included

This Timberdoodle curriculum kit is available in 3 different levels: Basic, Complete, and Elite. This allows you to choose the assortment best suited to your child's interest level, your family's schedule, and your budget. In this guide, you'll find an overview for each of the items included in the Elite Curriculum Kit, along with teaching tips. If you purchased a Basic or Complete kit, or if you customized your kit, you did not receive every item. Therefore, you'll only need to familiarize yourself with the items included in your kit.

Don't Panic—You Didn't Order Too Much Stuff!

We have yet to meet a homeschooler who doesn't have other irons in the fire. From homesteading or running a business to swimming lessons or doctor appointments, your weeks are not dull. As you unpack your box, you may be wondering how you'll fit it all in. We'll go in-depth on schedules momentarily, but for now, know that most of the items in your kit feature short lessons, and not all of them should be done every day or even every week. Your checklist (aka the weekly to-do list) is going to make this incredibly manageable. Really!

Tips & Tricks

Your First Week, State Laws, and More

It Gets Better!

As you get started this year, realize that you are just getting your sea legs. Expect your studies to take a little longer and be a little less smooth than they will be by the end of the year. As you get your feet under you, you will discover the rhythm that works best for you!

Find Your Pace

We asked parents who used this kit how long their students spent on "school," This grade encompassed quite a range—from 1-2 hours a day to 4-5 hours a day. That is a wide variation, and it also means some days were shorter or longer than that. Make sure to allow time to find a pace that is right for you and your student!

Books First or Not?

Some goal-oriented students might like to start each day with bookwork and end with fun, hands-on time. Others might prefer to intersperse the hands-on thinking games, STEM, and so forth between more intensive subjects to give their brains a clean slate. If you don't know where to begin each day, why not try starting with something from the Thinking Skills category? It will get your child's brain in gear and set a great tone for the rest of the day.

A Little Every Day, or All at Once?

Depending on your preferences, your child's attention span, and what other time commitments you have (teaching other children, doctor appointments, working around a baby's

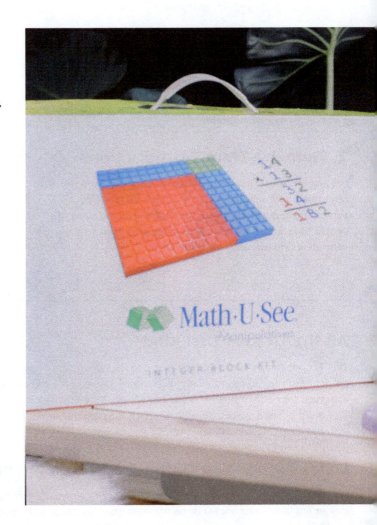

nap), there are many different ways to schedule your week. Some families like to do a little portion from nearly all subjects every day, while others prefer to blast out an entire week's work within a subject in a single sitting. Throughout the year, you can tinker around with your daily scheduling and see what approach works best for your family.

Tips for Newbies

If you're new to homeschooling, it might be helpful for you to know that some subjects are typically taught and practiced several times a week for the best mastery. These include basic math instruction, phonics, and spelling.

However, more topical subjects such as geography, history, and science are often taught all at once. Meanwhile, thinking skills, STEM, art, hands-on learning, and games can be even more tailored to the preferences of the child or used for independent learning while you are busy.

What about the Courses That You Don't Work on Every Week?

As you go over your checklist, you'll notice that some of your courses are "2–3 per month" or "as desired." That may leave you confused about how to tackle them. Here are a few options: You could go ahead and do it every week, completing the course early. You could set aside the item for summer. Or you could complete it as suggested, of course!

The Summer Plan

If you're looking at all these tools and feeling a little overwhelmed, or if you just wish you had more structured activities for the summer, feel free to grab a handful of items from the kit and set them aside for summer. Then set a reminder on your phone or calendar about which ones they are and where you stashed them so you won't forget to use them!

Meeting State Requirements

Check https://www.hslda.org/laws to see the most current information on your specific requirements. For many states, it is sufficient to hang on to your completed and dated weekly checklists along with a sampling of your child's best work this year. Some states ask you to add a state-specific topic, such as Vermont history, or a generic course like P.E. or health. We have a summary on our blog comparing your kit to state requirements, but HSLDA is the gold standard for current legal information.

P.E.? Health?

We suggest thinking outside the box on this. Many of the science courses have a health component that meets the requirement. P.E. is a great way to fit your child's favorite activity into the school schedule. Ballet, soccer, horseback riding, swimming...there are so many fun ways to check off P.E. this year.

Put Your Child in Charge

The weekly checklists are the framework of your week, designed for maximum flexibility. Just check off each item as you get it done, and you'll be able to see at a glance what you still need to do this week. (This is true of the daily checklists as well—just on a shorter schedule.) Many students even prefer to get all their work done early in the week and enjoy all their leisure time at once!

Do Hard Things and Easy Ones

Our family provides foster care for kids who need a safe place for a while. This has exposed us to a whole new world of hard days and stressful weeks. If your child is struggling today, you are not failing if you take a step back and have him start with his most calming project. For our crew, often that would be art or the reading challenge. You even have a little slush room in most subjects, so don't hesitate to trim the lessons short during a busy or challenging week or to pause schoolwork today for a complete reset and tackle it fresh tomorrow.

At the same time, you are not doing your child any favors if you never teach him how to work through a challenge. After all, you have hard days as a parent and still get up, drink your coffee, and jump back in. Be aware of your own tendency either to have your child buckle down and push through or to let him ease off completely, then work to provide a healthy balance for your child, particularly if he is in the process of healing.

Pro Tip

If you are using paper checklists, when you first get out a week's checklist, go ahead and check off all the things you don't need to do this week. For instance, if your child did a few extra pages of math last week or you are putting off all art kits until winter, check those off. Doesn't that feel better?

The Sample Schedules

We're including a sample annual planner on page 16, as well as sample weekly planners for each level of your kit, reflecting a typical 36-week school year. This lets you see at a glance how this might work for you, even before you get a moment to sit down at your computer and print your own custom-fitted schedule.

Photo: The Johanson Family

Why Use a Weekly Checklist?

Flexibility and Structure Unite

One of the primary concerns a new homeschooler faces is "How do I know I'm doing enough?" Your Timberdoodle kit gives you the structure you need for the year, but how do you break that down into a plan for your month, week, or day?

Pitfall 1: No Plan

We've seen 2 significant pitfalls over the years. The first is having no plan or consistency at all. Perhaps you start materials at random and then toss them aside if it gets tough or something else catches your eye. You end the year having made undefined progress, and your days often seem like a frustrating blur that leaves you counting the hours to bedtime.

Pitfall 2: Overscheduling

The other pitfall is to overschedule your life:
8:30 song
8:33 storytime
8:40 math lesson
8:50 thinking skills game
8:57 history book

In our experience, this approach makes your life exponentially more stressful. What if the baby has a blowout at 8:30? Or perhaps you finally get the long-anticipated return phone call that you need to take? Or even a scheduled interruption such as a swim lesson or doctor appointment? Any of these scenarios will add stress, which heavily impacts the tone of your school time.

The Cure?

Timberdoodle's checklist system offers the perfect mix of structure and flexibility. You'll go online and build your schedule using our exclusive Schedule Customizer. (More details on how to do that in a moment.) Then you'll work the plan each week.

Start with Blocks of Time

We highly recommend a building-block approach for your homeschool schedule. Think through all the things you want to do: one-on-one school, independent learning, read-aloud books, outdoor time, chores...then create a rhythm that sets you up for success. (Need inspiration? You can read more about our own schedule in the articles and resources section.)

Put Them Together

Now that you have the building blocks in place, you may know you want to tackle one-on-one school topics right after morning chores while the toddler plays. This plan will work well whether morning chores take forever today or your child wakes up early and races through them. It will even work if you're doing emergency clean-up at your normal start time!

Use Your Checklist

Now, grab your weekly checklist and begin checking things off. As you settle into a rhythm, you'll discover whether your child likes to ease into the day with his least intimidating subject or whether he is at his most focused then, so you'll be doing something more challenging. But no matter where you begin, you'll be checking off items from the list!

Check It Off!

Consider having your child check off items as he finishes them. Some students prefer to check things off online or have you do so, while other students thrive with a paper list that they can frequently reference.

It's OK to Stumble

If you are new to homeschooling, expect your first few weeks to be a bit of a blur. Even those of us who grew up homeschooling and are implementing the program we wrote find that it can take a good 3-6 weeks to feel that we've really settled into a new rhythm.

Rewards?

Make this process as fun for you and your student as you can. Our crew loves screen time, so once a week we have a family movie time for those with their school list done. But if screen time isn't your child's motivator, pick something that is. Visiting a special park? A field trip to the zoo? Game night? Dessert? You could even vary it each week. Just make sure that it is genuinely motivating, sustainable, and, ideally, fun for you as well!

Weeks Will Vary

As you settle in, you'll find that your weeks vary. Sometimes the weather is terrible, the lessons are fascinating, and the rest of your crew allows you a lot of time to focus in with one student. Other weeks the newborn has colic, the weather is tempting you outside, and library books must be raced through before they are due back. Don't stress! We suggest checking off the big 3 (language arts, math, thinking skills) each week and allowing the other subjects to shift as needed.

Because you're logging progress online, you'll be able to recalculate easily if you realize you need to redouble your efforts for the last 8 weeks of school. But in the meantime, embrace the flexibility that you have. Outside time = P.E. Library books = literacy. And that colicky newborn? Well, he just might be helping your other students learn to be kind, sacrificial caregivers or even curious learners who find their own entertainment. It's hard to overestimate those skills or pencil them into the plan, so just embrace them when they arrive even if you have to cross off a few of the art plans for the week.

Meet Your Online Schedule Customizer

Getting the Most Out of Your Planner

Newest Feature

Among the many behind-the-scenes improvements already completed and the bigger updates scheduled for spring, there is one new feature on the site that you'll want to know about now: You can now see at a glance which things you skipped in previous weeks. This will make catching up even easier!

Use the Customizer

Beginning on page 23, you'll find sample weekly checklists for Basic, Complete, and Elite kits. Before you photocopy 36 of them, though, take a moment to check out the online Schedule Customizer that came free with your kit. You can easily adjust your days and weeks of school and tweak the checklist to include exactly what you want. Plus, you'll be able to print your weekly checklists directly from the Schedule Customizer and even log your progress!

First Time?

You'll need to activate your account for the Schedule Customizer to get started. If you ordered from our website, head directly to schedule.timberdoodle.com and log in. Your activated kit will be waiting for you!

If you ordered through a school district or need to activate a different email address, click the button in the middle of the page to submit your activation code from the inside front page of this handbook + your order number and start scheduling!

Before you get started, you'll want to know 3 things:

Photo: The Chiavarios Family in the Midwest

1. How Many Weeks Will You Do School?

A standard school year is 36 weeks plus breaks. Some families prefer to expedite and complete the entire year in fewer weeks—a great option to get this year's school done before a baby arrives, for instance. Or perhaps your family, like ours, prefers to school year-round and keep that brain sharp. Do keep in mind any mandatory school days in your state. Here in Washington we are expected to do some sort of learning 180 days a year (36 five-day weeks).

2. When Do You Want to Start?

Any day is fair game! You may want to match your local school district, but you don't have to.

3. What Breaks Do You Want?

Thanksgiving, Christmas, winter break, spring break…you could also add weeks off for travel, visiting grandparents, or…

If you are using the weekly checklist, you typically don't need to take the time to enter a single-day break since most families prefer to work a little harder on the other days that week and not lose their stride. But if you're using the daily schedule, or if it's easier for you, feel free to add in partial-week breaks too!

Check Your End Date

A standard school schedule is often 40 weeks long, with 36 weeks of schoolwork + 4 weeks of breaks.

What Days Do You Want to Do School?

If you are using a weekly schedule only, don't worry about this setting! But if you prefer a daily checklist, this is the place to set a 4-day week or move all school from Wednesday to Saturday.

Choose Your Items

Now just pop that data into the Schedule Customizer and proceed to the subject-by-subject review. Under each subject, you'll see your kit's items loaded by default, and you'll also find options to add in items you already had on hand, add custom courses, change the subject color, etc.

Edit Items

If you're opting for the daily scheduler, you have some helpful fine-tuning options. Just click "Edit" on any particular course to select which days of the week the course will appear. This lets you do things like schedule history only on Wednesday because that is co-op day. Or you could schedule science only on Tuesday/Thursday and STEM on Monday/Friday so that science and STEM are never on the same day.

Pro Tip

You can also opt to exclude an item from certain weeks. This is useful if you already know that you want to save an art kit for May so that Grandma can do it with Andrew or if you don't want to break out the graphic novel until after Christmas since you've set it aside as a gift.

Front-Load vs. Back-Load

This setting lets you manually tell the Schedule Customizer what to do with lessons that don't fit neatly into the schedule. E.g., if you have 40 lessons to complete over 36 weeks of school, would you prefer to do the 4 extra lessons over the first 4 weeks of school, the last 4 weeks of school, or spread evenly throughout?

Each will default to "spread evenly," but there are 2 cases where it can be helpful to change it. If it is a course that increases in difficulty as your child progresses (e.g., a Smart Game), then it can make sense to front-load so that he doubles up on the easiest possible lessons. Or if it is an item that builds on other courses (e.g., Daily 6-Trait Writing's 25-week course), then back-loading can make the most sense so that your child has completed as much of the other introductory material as possible before beginning.

Add Custom Courses

Your course list is limited only by your imagination. Perhaps your friend created a custom curriculum you want to include, your family band practices weekly, or you need to include ballet since that's P.E. this year. You can add these by using "Add Course" at the end of the subject-by-subject review.

Schedule Summary

Look over your schedule summary and make sure that everything is the way you want it, then click "Save & Continue." Congratulations—your schedule is complete!

Go to Your Dashboard

Click "Checklist" to print your checklist or log your progress. More about that in a moment.

Make More Lists

If you have 1 student and 1 teacher, feel free to buzz past this idea. But if you have an extra teacher—perhaps your spouse, a grandparent, or even an older sibling—then this may simplify your life! Instead of putting all of your child's work on a single list, you could put only the subjects you will teach on your list and the remaining subjects on "Grandma's list" for her ease.

If you have twins or multiple students at the same grade level, you can also make multiple lists to best meet each student's needs.

Print Your Lists

From the checklist section you can choose to log your progress on the screen or print your checklists. (We prefer a printed checklist for ease of reference, but some of you may find electronic tracking easier. To print, click "Schedule Overview," then set your view options and either download or print your lists.

Here are a few settings you may tweak:

1. Weekly or Daily?

As we discussed already, we generally prefer a weekly schedule for the simple reason that our weeks are rarely without some anomaly. Off to the dentist Tuesday? You won't fall behind by taking a day off. Or perhaps you have Friday Robotics Camp for a couple of weeks and need to get all the week's work done over 4 days instead of 5. No problem! This approach also teaches time-management skills. (See the article on independent learning at the back of this handbook.)

However, we've heard from many of you that having a daily schedule, especially for the first month, is a real lifesaver. The daily option of the Schedule Customizer is programmed to split up the work as evenly as possible over the week, with the beginning of the week having any extra pages or lessons. (We all know that end-of-the-week doldrums are a real thing!)

2. Show Unit Range?

This feature sounds very data-y and not super helpful, but we think you just might love it. Instead of saying that you need to do 7 pages of thinking skills this week, check this box to have it remind you that you're on pages 50–56 this week. If you prefer extreme flexibility, leave this box unchecked. But if you're afraid of falling behind without knowing it, this box will be your hero.

3. Large-Font Edition

Want a large-font option? Just check the box. If you don't like how it looks, you can always come back and uncheck it.

That's It!

Click "Download" or "Print," and you'll be ready to get started in moments! We've heard from a number of you that you prefer to print out your entire year's worth of schedules and spiral bind them at the local print shop. This is a brilliant idea, but we suggest using the checklists for a few weeks first just to make sure you've fine-tuned it as you wish so that you can avoid doing that more than once!

Log Your Progress Online

You now have the ability to log your work as you go. Click "Progress" and log what you've done. As you complete portions, you'll see your progress bars fill in, showing a more tangible representation of your progress this year.

Your Sample Annual Planner

Curriculum	Lesson or Pages	= Per Week
Language Arts		
Language Smarts, Level D	318 pages	8-9 pages
Mosdos Literature Opal	30 weeks of work	1 week's work
Spelling You See, Level D	36 weeks	10 minutes a day
CursiveLogic	10 weeks + 14 practice pages	1 week's work or page
Daily 6-Trait Writing	25 weeks	1 week's work
Beginning Word Roots	27 lessons or reviews	1 lesson or review
Math		
Math-U-See	30 lessons	1 lesson
Möbi Math Game	unlimited	once a week
Wrap-Ups Multiplication	unlimited	once a week
Thinking Skills		
Critical & Creative 3	142 pages	4 pages
Smart Dog	60 challenges	1-2 challenges
Battle Sheep	unlimited	once a week
Chess: Once a Pawn a Time	23 chapters	twice a week
History & Social Studies		
The Story of the World 3	42 chapters	1-2 chapters
Disasters in History	8 stories	as desired
Famous Figures of the Early Modern Era	10 figures	1-2 a month

Curriculum	Lesson or Pages	= Per Week
Geography		
Skill Sharpeners Geography, Grade 3	132 pages	3-4 pages
Puzzleball Globe	unlimited	once a month
Science		
Discover! Science 3	75 lessons	2+ lessons
Dr. Bonyfide 1	108 pages	3 pages
STEM Learning		
GraviTrax Academy	66 models/challenges	2 models
Typing Instructor for Kids	unlimited	3 lessons
Emotional Intelligence		
Social Skills Activities for Today's Kids Ages 8-9	75 activities	2-3 activities
Art		
Paint-by-Number Museum Series	4 paintings	as desired
The Nature Explorer's Drawing Guide for Kids	40 sketches	1-2 sketches
Have I Got a Story For You! Baroque	12 lessons	1 lesson or its projects
Learning Tools		
Needoh Nice Cube	unlimited	as desired

What Is a Lesson?

Item-by-Item Specs

Beginning on page 33 you'll find a detailed overview of each item, including information about how we scheduled the work and why. If you're looking for a quick reference page to refresh your mind on what exactly "one lesson" means for any of your materials, then here you go!

Language Smarts

You'll find 318 colorful pages to complete in this book. Have your child complete 8-9 a week to stay on track. Since some pages have more writing than others, your child might be more successful completing 2 pages a day than finishing all 8 or 9 on Friday.

Spelling You See D

There are 36 lessons, each of which includes 5 days of work. Two tips: If your student struggles with writing, your day's lesson is complete after 10 minutes of work—your child does not need to finish the whole chunk. Also, if you're using a 4-day week or don't get to all 5 days of work in a week, it is expected that you will still count that lesson as complete at the end of the week and move to the next one.

Mosdos Literature

Do 1 week's work as found in the 30-week schedule beginning on page 101 in this handbook. (There are a few variations on page 37 to expand this to 36 weeks if you'd prefer.) We suggest completing the bulk of the workbook pages but skipping the writing since you'll be covering that with *Daily 6-Trait Writing*.

CursiveLogic

This course is laid out in an easy-to-use 10-week plan. Complete 1 week's work every week until you're done. (Each week includes 3-4 days of work, with multiple pages per day.) We suggest beginning your school year with this course and then using cursive where appropriate throughout the year. There are also 14 practice pages for use after completing the course. We suggest 1 page a week for weeks 11–24.

Daily 6-Trait Writing

The course is split into 25 weeks of work. We suggest starting the pace of 1 week's work per week after 11 weeks of school to allow you to ease into the year.

Beginning Word Roots

You'll find 24 lessons clearly marked, each ranging from 2 to 4 pages. There are also 3 review chapters. We suggest completing 1 entire lesson or review each week, knowing you'll either finish 9 weeks early or have the flexibility to split a lesson 9 times.

Math-U-See

You'll find 30 lessons here, each with 7 worksheets. Since you'll be completing only as many of the worksheets as your child needs per lesson, and since completing 1 whole lesson a week keeps the instructional portions predictable, we suggest doing 1 lesson a week instead of a certain number of worksheets. If you use that method, know that you can spread a tricky lesson over 2 weeks up to 6 times this year without messing up your schedule.

Photo: The Haynes Family Overseas

Möbi Game

Unlimited. We suggest at least 1-2 games a week.

Wrap-Ups Multiplication

Unlimited. We suggest having your child use this once a week, racing his previous time, until it becomes too easy for him.

Critical and Creative

The simplest way to schedule this is to plan on 4 pages a week. If you prefer to work with units, complete 1-2 units a week.

Smart Dog Game

Just do 1-2 new challenges a week.

Battle Sheep

This game is unlimited. We suggest breaking it out at least once a week and playing a few rounds.

Chess Once a Pawn a Time

This game is unlimited. We suggest breaking it out at least once a week and playing a few rounds.

Photo: Brayden and Ella in Michigan

The Story of the World 3

With 42 chapters, you're going to want to do 3 chapters every 2 weeks. Or, if it's easier, just do 2 chapters one week and 1 chapter the following week. Add in as many activities as you have the time/interest for.

Disasters in History

Release it to your child at any point for free reading, or assign a book a week to read and discuss. Each of the 8 disasters is incredibly captivating!

Famous Figures of the Early Modern Era

There are 10 models to complete, each with a full-color and a color-it-yourself option. See the notes beginning on page 55 for assistance with integrating them into the most appropriate lessons.

Skill Sharpeners Geography

Completing 4 pages a week will get you through this year. Keep in mind that you're free to skip the writing assignments and elaborate activities if needed, but if your student has the time and energy, these will really serve to reinforce what he's learning.

Puzzleball Globe

Unlimited. We suggest your child complete it once a month or so until he has it mastered.

Discover! Science

Complete just over 2 lessons a week in order to finish this year. Each review is also labeled as a lesson; a fact that is helpful to know when scheduling.

Dr. Bonyfide 1

About 3 pages a week will take you through this year.

GraviTrax Academy

Gravitrax Deluxe includes 33 suggested models to build. We suggest 1 per week starting with the exact replication manual.

In the Gravitrax Game you have 30 challenges to solve, so we recommend completing 1 of those every week as well.

Typing Instructor for Kids

You decide. The more time you allow, the more skills your student will gain. We'd suggest 3 lessons a week, but fine-tune that for your student.

Paint-by-Number Museum Series

There are 4 great paintings to complete. At this age, most students will want to save these for days when they will have enough time to totally complete one. Work that in as desired.

Photo: The W. Family in Texas

Have I Got a Story for You!

The *Have I Got a Story for You!* art program is truly one-of-a-kind. It is designed with 12 lessons, and each lesson includes a video as well as art assignments. We suggest watching the video the first week and completing 1 of the related art projects on the 2 following weeks. Many third-graders will want to repeat the video at least once more, so please do that as time allows!

The Nature Explorer's Drawing Guide for Kids

With 40 sketches, complete 1-2 a week. If you are using a typical 36-week school year, just plan on having your child complete the extra sketches during a break or when you need a bit time for him to be working independently.

NeeDoh Nice Cube

Unlimited. We suggest pulling this out the first week of school so that your child has a fidget handy. Use it throughout the year to keep his hands busy so his mind can think.

Test Prep

We usually save this for the end of the year to refresh the student on all the skills he'll need for annual testing. You won't find this on your schedule unless you add it.

Photo: The Belter Family on the Oregon Coast

Sample Weekly Checklist

Basic

Curriculum	This Week	Check It Off!

Language Arts

Curriculum	This Week	Check It Off!
Language Smarts, Level D	8-9 pages	☐ ☐ ☐ ☐ ☐ ☐ ☐ ☐ ☐
Mosdos Literature Opal	1 week's work	☐
Spelling You See, Level D	10 minutes a day	☐ ☐ ☐ ☐
CursiveLogic	1 week's work or page	☐

Math

Curriculum	This Week	Check It Off!
Math-U-See	1 lesson	☐

Thinking Skills

Curriculum	This Week	Check It Off!
Critical & Creative 3	4 pages	☐ ☐ ☐ ☐

Sample Weekly Checklist

Complete

Curriculum	This Week	Check It Off!
Language Arts		
Language Smarts, Level D	8-9 pages	
Mosdos Literature Opal	1 week's work	
Spelling You See, Level D	10 minutes a day	
CursiveLogic	1 week's work or page	
Daily 6-Trait Writing	1 week's work	
Math		
Math-U-See	1 lesson	
Möbi Math Game	once a week	
Wrap-Ups Multiplication	once a week	
Thinking Skills		
Critical & Creative 3	4 pages	
Smart Dog	1-2 challenges	
History & Social Studies		
The Story of the World 3	1-2 chapters	
Disasters in History	as desired	

Geography

Skill Sharpeners Geography, Grade 3	3-4 pages	

Science

Discover! Science	2+ lessons	
Dr. Bonyfide 1	3 pages	

STEM Learning

GraviTrax Academy	2 models	
Typing Instructor for Kids	3 lessons	

Art

Paint-by-Number Museum Series	as desired	
The Nature Explorer's Drawing Guide for Kids	1-2 sketches	

Sample Weekly Checklist

Elite

Curriculum	This Week	Check It Off!
Language Arts		
Language Smarts, Level D	8-9 pages	☐ ☐ ☐ ☐ ☐ ☐ ☐ ☐ ☐
Mosdos Literature Opal	1 week's work	☐
Spelling You See, Level D	10 minutes a day	☐ ☐ ☐ ☐ ☐
CursiveLogic	1 week's work or page	☐
Daily 6-Trait Writing	1 week's work	☐ ☐ ☐ ☐
Beginning Word Roots	1 lesson or review	☐
Math		
Math-U-See	1 lesson	☐
Möbi Math Game	once a week	☐
Wrap-Ups Multiplication	once a week	☐
Thinking Skills		
Critical & Creative 3	4 pages	☐ ☐ ☐ ☐
Smart Dog	1-2 challenges	☐
Battle Sheep	once a week	☐
Chess: Once a Pawn a Time	twice a week	☐ ☐
History & Social Studies		
The Story of the World 3	1-2 chapters	☐ ☐
Disasters in History	as desired	☐
Famous Figures of the Early Modern Era	1-2 a month	☐

Geography

Skill Sharpeners Geography, Grade 3	3-4 pages	☐☐☐☐
Puzzleball Globe	once a month	☐

Science

Discover! Science	2+ lessons	☐☐
Dr. Bonyfide 1	3 pages	☐☐

STEM Learning

GraviTrax Academy	2 models	☐☐
Typing Instructor for Kids	3 lessons	☐☐

STEM Learning

Social Skills Activities for Today's Kids Ages 8-9	2-3 activities	☐☐

Art

Paint-by-Number Museum Series	as desired	☐
The Nature Explorer's Drawing Guide for Kids	1-2 sketches	☐
Have I Got a Story For You! Baroque	1 lesson or its projects	☐

Introducing the Reading Challenge

Third Grade: Early Modern History

The Reading Challenge for kids will get you and your child reading a broader variety of books this year while covering essential topics.

Your reading challenge introduces 36 different weekly topics to explore together. Choose a book off your library shelf and check off the subject, or go deep with multiple books and activities. Do whatever works for you this week, flexing for at-home weeks with more time to fill and on-the-go weeks that need no extra activities.

At this grade level, your child will read some of these books independently, and you will read many together. Don't be too eager to lose the one-on-one reading time either. Many sources recommend that parents continue reading to their children well past the time they become accomplished readers, and we agree!

Reading Together

Most of us probably have a deep sense that reading to kids is a good choice. But do you know why?

There are dozens of appealing reasons, but let me just remind you of the 3 highlighted by the American Academy of Pediatrics (AAP):

1. Strengthen language skills
2. Build literacy development and interest in reading
3. Create nurturing parent-child relationships, which are "important for a child's cognitive, language, and social-emotional development"

Photo: The Pers Family in the Dutch Caribbean

1. Language Skills

Reading exposes your child to familiar and unfamiliar words, scenes, and feelings as you give words to each of them. As he gets older and the books become more complex, he'll also be learning syntax, pronunciation, rhyming, and more!

2. Literacy Development

Your child is seeing that books are engaging and important to you. You are also demonstrating that they are interesting and a worthy use of time. This is such critical knowledge!

3. Nurturing Parent-Child Relationships

Surely we aren't the only ones who have stared at our darling child feeling like we have already done all the things and wondering how in the world we will fill the remaining time in the day. What if instead of screen time or pleading with him to play by himself, you reached happily for a book? Can you imagine how much bonding and conversation could fill in the gaps of your day?

Now, we know all too well that there are moments when children do need to play independently, for both your sanity and theirs. And if you're blessed with more than one little one (as our family is), you can't sit and read as much of the day as you'd prefer. But every minute of reading you squeeze in cultivates your relationship with your precious child without much in-the-moment effort on your part!

4. Emotional Intelligence

We've added this point to the AAP's list. Emotional intelligence is a critical skill yet challenging to teach. Reading together is an easy way to teach emotional intelligence in an unlimited variety of contexts. This not only helps your child become more fluent in his own feelings but also develops empathy and understanding for the people around him.

How It Works

On each week's challenge page (beginning on page 110), you'll find 3 things:
- A list of suggested book titles
- A place to write in the titles you read together
- A chart to track your progress through the reading challenge.

You will set your own pace this year, ranging from 1 to 5 books per week. Choose a reading goal early in the year and set your pace accordingly, keeping in mind what is realistic for your family this year.

Here's the pace for a 36-week schedule:

- Light Reader: 1 book every week (36 total)
- Interested Reader: 2 books every week (72 total)
- Avid Reader: 3 books every week (108 total)
- Committed Reader: 4 books every week (144 total)
- Enthralled Reader: 5 books every week (180 total)

But I Don't Have Any Idea Which Books to Choose!

We have your back! Beginning on page 112 you'll find thousands of book ideas you'll love this year.

If you want more ideas, we highly recommend your local librarian, the Read-Aloud Revival podcast, and the Timberdoodle Facebook groups as excellent starting points. It's also a wonderful idea to peek at the additional reading ideas in your history or science textbooks—particularly if your child found he was fascinated by something his courses recently touched on.

What about Reading Level?

This year we're providing you with a range of titles. Many are are designed for early readers while others range from chapter books designed to be read to your child to picture books to enjoy together. Pick and choose the titles and styles you think will work best for your child, but we'd also suggest adding a few books to your library list from outside your normal selection. (E.g., if your child gravitates to books he can read himself, make sure you also include some more complex books for you to read aloud.) Why? Children rarely enjoy only one type of book. They just may not know what they like yet! In light of that, we highly encourage you to intentionally expose your child to a broad spectrum of literature and see what stands out to you both.

Will This Be Expensive?

It doesn't need to be. You can read library books and e-books, buy used, borrow from friends, and scour your family bookshelves. Don't forget that many libraries have free e-books as well. If you have Kindle Unlimited or Everand, check for these titles there also. It doesn't get much more convenient than that!

Before You Begin

Please note that you do not need to complete these challenges in order! We highly recommend using the seasonal ones as close to the appropriate holiday as your schedule allows. Or if your child is all about reptiles this week, there is no need to wait until week 21 to study them.

It is also OK to skip or substitute topics. Perhaps your child is well-versed in farms but would love to learn about specific artists. Or on a deeper level, some of our young children in foster care would enjoy books about family, while others would find them triggering. It's totally appropriate to substitute a book about wild animal parents or whatever makes it more appropriate and interesting for your child.

Extra Activities

On the following pages you'll find additional ideas our team has brainstormed that may be helpful for your family. If you're looking for field trip ideas, art inspiration, or a theme for the week, use these. If your week is quite busy enough, skip them! They are not essential—just bonus ideas if you have extra time this week or want to meet a field trip goal.

Let's Read!

Pick your plan, choose some books with your child, and get started!

Looking for more reading challenges? Check out RedeemedReader.com and Challies.com for their original versions of this reading challenge. It has been completely remodeled by us over the years but was initially inspired by them and used with permission.

A Fun Beginning-of-the-Year Interview

Have your student jot down his answers here to capture a fun time capsule of his third-grade year.

What do you want to do when you grow up?

Who are some people you would like to learn something from?

Do you want to play an instrument? If so, which one(s)?

What is your favorite food to make? To eat?

What's the most important, longest, or most interesting thing you've memorized?

What is your favorite subject to learn?

What makes you laugh? (Or who?)

What activities does your family like to do (as individuals or together)?

Where is your favorite place?

Item-by-Item Introductions

Language Arts

Grammar, Literature, Writing, Spelling, and Cursive

Reading is probably the most important skill your child will practice this year. Whether he is a natural reader or doesn't enjoy reading, it is critical to make reading as fun and rewarding as possible now.

Our experience is that the best way to cultivate an eager reader is to constantly supply him with reading materials that interest him. Future doctors may want to read up on anatomy, young explorers are drawn to the escapades of adventurers young and old, and the baby-lover in your family will be captivated by adoption stories.

We're also including a brilliant anthology of reading material in your Mosdos book this year. With so many excellent selections, every student is sure to find some that resonate deeply with him and others that he would never have chosen for himself but that he finds surprisingly interesting. Assign reading as needed this year, but encourage it at all costs; a child who enjoys reading will find it easier to excel in every area.

A Note about Writing

Take a good look at your child's abilities and writing readiness before insisting that he complete all of the written portions, particularly of Mosdos. Here are the writing assignments you can anticipate this year.

Language Smarts

The emphasis here is on grammar, and most pages are fast-paced and colorful. However, there are some that do require a fair amount of writing. Most third-graders are ready for this intensity, but if yours is not, feel free to spread them over multiple days or ask your child to answer every other prompt on the page.

Spelling You See

The motor movements of physically writing will help your child retain the spelling he's learning here. It's designed to be used for only 10 minutes a day, so it shouldn't be overwhelming.

Mosdos Press Literature

We love this for its literature. Isn't it beautiful? However, you're already covering writing, so we highly recommend skipping the writing activities in the student reader. The student workbook (and possibly the oral review questions) is great for reading comprehension, so do that. Just skip the writing or allow oral answers.

CursiveLogic

We'd encourage you to consider prioritizing this even if your child is a reluctant writer. Learning cursive has some real benefits that may help make the rest of his writing easier (see page 38).

Daily 6-Trait Writing

Each lesson is wonderfully short, and this course doesn't even begin until the 12th week of school. Winner!

Language Smarts

==Basic== | ==Complete== | ==Elite==

Language Smarts is a complete language arts curriculum that will improve your student's reading, writing, spelling, punctuation, and grammar skills. But unlike a traditional workbook, *Language Smarts* also employs both convergent and divergent thinking in its exercises.

Perfect for the child who prefers to work independently, *Language Smarts* pages are brightly colored and contain enough white space to feel easily doable.

About 2 pages a day will have your student completing *Language Smarts* within a school year.

Language Smarts proves that studying language arts does not have to include the predictably intensive, tedious, and repetitive activities found in most traditional language arts workbooks.

Instead, *Language Smarts* uses rhymes and riddles, editing challenges, mind-benders, sequencing, and more. The simple, colorful exercises can make this the year your child enjoys language arts.

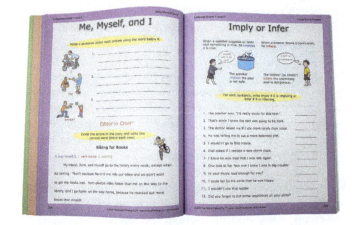

Scheduling

With 318 pages, just complete 8-9 a week to stay on track.

Spelling You See, Level D

Basic | Complete | Elite

This multisensory spelling program will help your child become a confident, successful speller, naturally and at his own speed. Because *Spelling You See* encourages visual memory rather than rote memory, there are no weekly spelling lists or tests and very little instructor preparation. Each daily lesson in *Spelling You See: Americana* uses real words presented in context within nursery rhymes and interesting nonfiction passages about animals.

Spelling You See: Americana is colorful, short, to the point, and fun!

Scheduling

The 36 weeks of work, with 5 daily activities each week, are already planned out for you. Just open and go!

Pro Tip

Never spend more than 10 minutes on spelling in a day. There is enough work in each lesson to keep a speedy writer busy for the whole 10 minutes, but a more methodical writer would be overwhelmed trying to complete it all. We highly encourage you to start a timer when you begin the day's work and stop where you are when it rings. The next day, just move on to the new lesson.

Mosdos Press Literature

Basic | Complete | Elite

Mosdos Press Literature is a complete literature program that cheerily reinforces the universal ideals of courage, honesty, loyalty, and compassion. We found this such a breath of fresh air in comparison to more sensational stories that glamorize evil or present subject matter that is not age appropriate.

Mosdos Literature begins with the student readers, which are beautifully illustrated using a generous number of full-color photographs, color drawings, and black-and-white pictures. Your student will complete the *Sunflower Reader* first, then move on to the *Daisy Reader*.

Before each story in the student reader, there is an introduction to the story and an explanation of some facet of literature. That literary focus can include character, theme, internal and external conflicts, setting, climax, foreshadowing, and more. This literary component is developed and illuminated through the stories. Vocabulary words that might be unfamiliar are presented in boxes on the pages where the words first appear in the account.

The stories are followed not just by classic review questions designed to assess reading comprehension but also by more complex questions that require thoughtful analysis. Every unit concludes with activities such as writing a short skit, doing a craft, or memorizing a poem. Pick the ones that best suit your child; there are far too many to do them all. Unless your child is a budding author, you can minimize the writing activities. Your child is already doing a lot of writing this year in *Daily 6–Trait Writing* and *Language Smarts*.

Next is the consumable, colorful, and engaging student activity workbook. For nearly every story in the student reader, the workbook contains corresponding vocabulary, creative writing, or comprehension questions, while also providing extended reinforcement of the literary elements being taught. These assignments help you to evaluate areas of progress or concepts that might require additional work.

The advantage of Mosdos Press is that the literature, vocabulary, and application components tie together, giving your child a chance to truly understand what was taught by approaching it in a variety of ways.

Through great commentary plus questions and answers, the teacher's edition will make lively discussions with your child possible. Each page of the student reader is duplicated at a smaller size in the teacher's edition, yet it is still abundantly easy to read. Information is arranged in the ample margins around these replicated pages, discussing the literary components found in each story with clear, concise explanations. Of course, the teacher's edition also includes the answers for the student activity workbook.

Scheduling

Don't worry! This is easier to use than it appears at first glance. A detailed explanation is below for those of you who prefer to get all the details. If you just want to know what to do this week, pop over to page "Mosdos Opal Weekly Assignments" on page 101 for a week-by-week schedule.

Here are the nitty-gritty details: you have 6 units in the course, all helpfully labeled in the teacher's edition. A typical unit is further broken down into 5 subsections for daily assignments.

A week's work will typically begin with the Lesson in Literature and include reading until you reach the next Lesson in Literature.

Our family would have chosen to answer the Studying the Selection questions in the readers orally. If time allowed, we might have selected 1 Focus or Creating and Writing activity to complete for further study. In most cases, however, we suggest skipping the writing since you'll be covering that with *Daily 6-Trait Writing*.

Note that the last unit in the book, "A Toad for Tuesday," looks a bit different visually and comprises 3 weeks' work.

Busy families may choose to skip the Unit Wrap-Ups, while others who enjoy the hands-on activities can complete them.

This course naturally breaks into 30 sections or weeks of work, 5 per unit. If you have a traditional 36-week school year, you have several fantastic options:

1. Take a week off after each unit
2. Move the Unit Wrap-Ups to a week of their own.
3. Would you perhaps prefer to finish early?
4. Or use the 6 extra weeks as free passes for particularly hectic weeks.

You decide!

Pro Tip

The student activity workbook is double-sided. Just flip it over to get to the other half of the book!

CursiveLogic

Basic | Complete | Elite

Research now reports a clear connection between handwriting and language, as well as between memory and critical thinking skills. A student who takes notes by hand performs better than students who take notes on laptops, both in understanding and recall. Moreover, writing letters (especially in cursive) as opposed to viewing them on a screen is associated with more advanced brain function.

If you have a child who struggles with learning cursive, then *CursiveLogic* may be just what you need. Using a multi-sensory approach with 4 basic shapes, *CursiveLogic* will teach your child proper formation and connection for all letters in just 10 weeks.

Rather than teaching each letter individually, *CursiveLogic* teaches all the letters that share a common shape at once. Each group of letters is color-coded to help your student readily recall the initial strokes as he learns them; bright orange, lime green, silver, and mauve capture students' attention. Using colored pencils and pens can add even more to the learning and the fun.

However, when your child has advanced to tracing and writing words that combine letters from different groups, he should not stop and switch writing instruments in the middle of a word to match the color coding. It is more important that he learn to write continuously at that stage, so he'll need to use just 1 color.

CursiveLogic includes information about grip, body and hand placement, suggestions for left-handed students, and more.

Scheduling

This book is designed as a 10-week course, and we think you'll see maximum impact by using it that way. We'd suggest starting your year with this one as your child will then be able to use his new skills for the rest of his school year. Plus, you'll finish *CursiveLogic* just a week before beginning *Daily 6-Trait Writing*, which makes it easy on your schedule.

You'll quickly notice that each week includes 3-4 days of work, with multiple pages per day. This is intentional, and it is paced to build maximum skills. You'll just want to flex the rest of your student's workload around it.

Also, you'll find 14 practice pages to complete after finishing the course. We suggest 1 a week to keep your student's skills sharp.

Daily 6-Trait Writing

~~Basic~~ | Complete | Elite

Are you familiar with trait writing? Trait-based writing is an impressive method that educators have developed to determine whether a child's writing is skilled or not.

The 6 traits or characteristics that shape quality writing are content; organization; word choice; sentence fluency; voice; and conventions, which include grammar, spelling, and mechanics. It may sound ominous, but *Daily 6-Trait Writing* has made it effortless.

These short daily assignments are designed to build skills without being overwhelming. We love them for their brevity but also because they are so thorough!

Scheduling

Includes 25 weeks of work, which we suggest implementing as 1 short lesson a day, beginning on week 12 of school.

We suggest you begin when your student is ready. If you start later in the year, you'll find that the "extra" pages make great review in the summer to keep his brain sharp.

If you have a student who struggles with fine motor skills, you may have more success if you completely separate writing skills from motor skills. Most families do this by allowing their students to dictate their writing, but you could also use a whiteboard (bigger writing may be easier) or allow your student to use a computer or tablet/phone. That enables your child to build fantastic writing skills, even while his motor skills are still developing.

Beginning Word Roots

~~Basic~~ | ~~Complete~~ | Elite

Children who have a solid grasp of word roots are bound to have better reading comprehension skills, primarily because they have acquired the ability to decode words.

It may not surprise you, then, to hear that according to national standards, students in grades 4-12 must now be able to demonstrate their knowledge of how to use common Greek and Latin roots for analyzing the meaning of complex words.

Learning word elements also dramatically improves spelling and the ability to decode unfamiliar words. The Word Roots series will add hundreds of words to your child's vocabulary and greater depth to his thinking and writing.

Your child will be getting a jump start this year with *Beginning Word Roots*. It will teach your child the meanings of Latin prefixes, roots, and suffixes of words commonly used in English without much effort. Just grab the workbook and go!

Scheduling

With 24 lessons plus 3 review chapters, we suggest completing 1 lesson or review chapter a week. This will either let you finish 9 weeks early or allow you to defer or split a lesson up to 9 times. However, if you prefer to work by page count, just do about 3 pages a week.

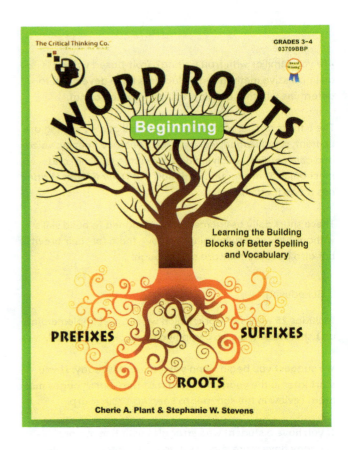

Mathematics

A Fundamental Skill

Basic math is a critical skill for your child to master, whether he grows up to be a carpenter, doctor, accountant, or farmer. But all too often math programs rely on memorization instead of comprehension, leaving the student at a disadvantage.

That's not going to happen to your child! The real-world math problems posed in Math-U-See (combined with the hands-on manipulatives) create an unbeatable math program.

With simple, uncluttered pages, Math-U-See is mastery-oriented, clear, to the point, and effective. In Math-U-See, new ideas are introduced step by step in a logical order, while concepts that have been mastered are reviewed periodically.

Math-U-See's teacher guide and supplemental DVD will teach more than just how to solve a math problem. They will also show why the problem is solved in this manner and when to apply the concept. On the DVDs, each lesson is demonstrated with kind-hearted enthusiasm. DVDs can be played on a DVD player or computer; however, Windows 10 users will need to download a separate video player.

Math-U-See

Basic | Complete | Elite

Math-U-See does require a fair amount of parental involvement. Thankfully, the maker of this math program has bent over backward to make the lesson planning as painless as possible. Still, at this grade, feel free to merely skim the teacher's guide, as it is pretty straightforward.

One Math-U-See lesson is designed to consist of several parts:

- A video lesson

- Worksheet A, teaching this lesson's concept

- Worksheet B, teaching this lesson's concept, in case your student needs a bit more practice

- Worksheet C, still teaching this lesson's concept, in case your student needs even more practice

- Worksheet D, review work

- Worksheet E, more review work

- Worksheet F, still more review work, for the student who thrives on repetition or struggles with math and requires the extra practice

- Worksheet G is often a test or optional application and enrichment section. While it is considered "honors" material, we suggest you do this if you can tackle it without stressing your child!

Some parents prefer to watch the lessons themselves and then teach their students personally, while most prefer to watch alongside their students, pausing the video, rewinding, and clarifying as needed.

After watching the video lesson or your recreated lesson, your student will complete as many worksheets as you deem appropriate. You will want to decide as you start the year whether your student will be completing the optional "Application and Enrichment" section on each lesson (sometimes considered the honors portion).

It's hard to overemphasize the importance of thoughtfully assigning math pages. Most students should complete worksheets A, D, and G, and that may be enough! In our crew, we have some students who struggle with math, and for them it is best to complete most of the worksheets and just slow down the pace of the program. This is perfectly acceptable but shouldn't be the norm for every child since the only thing worse than being overwhelmed by rapid-fire challenging concepts is being bored with too much repetition!

Scheduling

You have 30 lessons to complete, so we suggest planning on 1 lesson a week, including the DVD as well as the textbook/ workbook portions and any relevant tests. However, as Mr. Demme points out, some lessons will take you longer than others to achieve mastery. If you find yourself stuck on a lesson, feel free to allow it to take you an extra week. Just don't do that more than 6 times this year!

Photo: The Amisi Family in Kenya

Wrap-Ups Multiplication

~~Basic~~ | Complete | Elite

Even though math should never be just a drill, it is a rare child who would not benefit from some drill work. Wrap-Ups are convenient, portable, self-contained, and, best of all, self-correcting!

Your child can use Wrap-Ups in the car, at the beach, at the doctor's office, or even during a homeschool meeting; the possibilities are endless! Wrap-Ups are excellent for drill-work. Challenge your child to complete a board in less than a minute before he starts the next board.

Each set of Wrap-Ups contains 10 self-correcting, joined-at-the-top boards (about 1½"x5"), with a colorful attached string. The string wraps around from the problem on the left to the answer on the right. If the answers are correct, the string will cover the lines on the back of the board.

This is a wonderful tool for visual and kinesthetic learners. If you encourage your child to say the problems aloud, it is equally marvelous for the auditory child. Because it is self-correcting, your child will have immediate feedback for checking accuracy (plus it takes you out of the picture as the bearer of "bad news").

Scheduling

Start using these Wrap-Ups after your child has learned the concept of multiplication. We suggest getting this set out at least once a week until he has mastered it.

Möbi Math Game

~~Basic~~ | Complete | Elite

Multiply your child's math calculation speed while adding fun to his day with Möbi Math. This fast-paced number tile game transforms necessary math drill from tedious to exciting. Möbi's crossword-style game is made up of sturdy aqua blue number tiles and white double-sided operations tiles. Use them to make simple math equations of addition, subtraction, multiplication, and division. But make them fast, because the first player to use all of his blue tiles and yell "Möbi" wins.

Begin by separating the colors into 2 piles, with the number tiles face down. Draw 7 number tiles. Operations tiles are taken as needed, and you can use either side of the tile. Then, as fast as possible, create a "pod" of math equations to use up your number tiles. As you play, you will be adding more number tiles to your pile until all tiles from the pool are gone. To integrate newly drawn tiles, you will often need to rearrange existing tiles, so your pod is always shifting. The first player who completes his pod wins.

Scheduling

This game is truly unlimited. We suggest breaking it out once a week and playing a game or 2 to keep your child's skills sharp.

Photo: The Lahtis in Eastern Washington

There are many ways to play Möbi, but here are a few of our favorite variations:

Add & Subtract

Use only the addition and subtraction tiles for the entire game.

Chill Möbi

Divide all the number tiles evenly among the players at the start of the game.

Number of the Day

Pick a number, then every player must include that number somewhere in each of his equations.

My Number Is _____

Every player has his own "number of the day" and must use it in every equation.

On My Pod

Every player is given a sum for 1 of his problems. (Make every player's the same or use bigger numbers for those who need more of a challenge.) Each player must keep that sum in his pod at all times.

Mandatory Multiplication

If your student is ready for more of a challenge, or if you really want to work on multiplication skills, require him to use at least 1 multiplication (or division) tile in every equation.

Thinking Skills

This Is as Critical as It Is Appealing

In Timberdoodle's curriculum kits, you will find a rigorous pursuit of thinking skills for every child, in every grade. This is not an optional skill for your child. A child who can think logically will be able to learn well and teach himself in ways that an untrained brain will find difficult.

Be thankful that you won't have to persuade your child to learn to think, though—he's wired for problem-solving! We're guessing this portion of the curriculum will be the hardest not to race through. After all, who doesn't want to work through a creative thinking skills puzzle book, solve the puzzle of his dog's obstacles, or beat you in a quick round of Battle Sheep?

Critical & Creative

Basic | Complete | Elite

It is nearly impossible to overemphasize thinking skills when planning a child's education. A student who doesn't know how to think things through will be at a disadvantage in every area of study.

This course specifically features the relationship between critical and creative thought. While often misunderstood, profound thinking requires both imagination and intellectual ideas. To produce excellence in thinking, we need to engage our children in a curriculum that overlaps the logical and imaginative sides of thinking.

Critical & Creative's 46 theme-based units will give your child lots of practice thinking in a variety of ways. From brainteasers and logic puzzles to mazes, Venn diagrams, and secret codes, *Critical & Creative Thinking Activities* has a wealth of mind-boggling activities that your child will enjoy while he learns thinking fluency, originality, generalizing, patterning, and problem-solving.

Scheduling

The simplest way to schedule this is to complete 4 pages a week. This also gives you the advantage of being able to pull pages out of the book to assign them!

Some families will prefer to complete 1-2 units a week so that you don't lose the continuity of doing all the pages on a certain topic at once.

Smart Dog

~~Basic~~ | Complete | Elite

Corgis can tackle obstacle courses with ease, showcasing their agility, intelligence, and boundless energy. Watching them zip through jumps, tunnels, and weave poles is not only adorable but also impressive!

Now your child can create a colorful path for his pup to run through with Smart Dog. This visually appealing game uses the theme of a dog agility course that includes various colored obstacles, such as a bridge, tubes, and a hoop. The Corgi travels in a straight line until an obstacle changes its direction.

As your child designs obstacle courses for his Corgi, he'll not only be entertained but will also hone his logic, spatial insight, and problem-solving abilities. So unleash his creativity, and watch as his pup's skills—and his own—reach new heights!

Scheduling

There are 60 challenges from easy to im-paws-ible, so plan on completing 1-2 a week.

Battle Sheep

~~Basic~~ | ~~Complete~~ | Elite

Opposing sheep herds are battling it out to secure the most pastureland in a strategy game that your whole family will love. Battle Sheep's tactical gameplay requires a player to think through his moves at least 2 steps ahead, or the open pasture will quickly become filled with rival sheep, and he will be fenced out.

Using both offensive and defensive moves, the player who captures the most pasture space wins the game.

Easy to learn and easy to play without being easy to win, Battle Sheep's ever-changing pasture boards allow for different and unique game-playing areas each time. Your students can play several games in less than an hour, providing them multiple opportunities to apply new strategies from their previous game.

A very durable game with high-quality components, Battle Sheep's 16 pasture boards are made of laminated cardstock. The 64 sheep tokens are made of thick plastic.

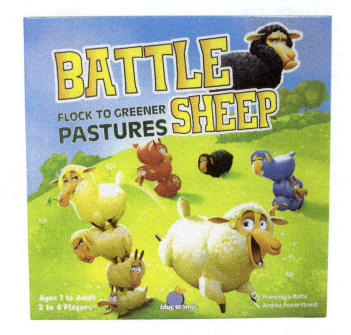

(Scheduling)

Unlimited. We suggest playing as many rounds as you like at least once a week.

Chess Once a Pawn a Time

~~Basic~~ | ~~Complete~~ | Elite

Back in the '80s, when Timberdoodle was just launched, homeschoolers were known for their denim jumpers, wheat grinders, and love of chess. Fast forward nearly 40 years, and our fashion sense and household expectations have improved, but our passion for chess is just as strong.

If your family has ever felt this social influence to play chess or you want some of the proven benefits of chess—strengthening academic performance, sharpening critical thinking, and boosting emotional intelligence—then Once a Pawn a Time is a great place to start. This imaginative approach to teaching chess is the most straightforward method we have ever seen.

Your child will fully understand each piece and its permitted moves at the completion of this course. Even if you have never played chess yourself, Once a Pawn a Time is all you need to teach your child and yourself this classic game.

Once a Pawn a Time includes 2 instructional books. The first book whimsically introduces the chess pieces, the 2 chess kingdoms, and the board layout. The second book builds on those foundational skills by exploring the strengths and weaknesses of each chess piece, strengthening your child's novice playing abilities.

Along with these books, the set also includes a folding chess board and a complete set of pieces, providing your child with everything he needs to enjoy the game for years to come.

We can't wait for your child to embark on their chess journey with Once a Pawn a Time!

Scheduling

Unlimited. We suggest playing as many rounds as you like at least twice a week. Also, plan to introduce a new chapter from the book every week or so. You have about 23 chapters total to explore together.

History & Social Studies

Many history curriculum options make the mistake of focusing solely on U.S. history. As important as that is, doesn't it make more sense to start with the big picture of history? This year you'll learn about the early modern times, covering the major historical events in the years 1600–1850, from Elizabeth I to the Forty-Niners. You'll answer questions like these:

- Who was the Sun King?

- What was the Black Hole of Calcutta?

- Why was a California town named Groundhog Glory?

- And, of course, how did samurai become sumo wrestlers?

With *Disasters in History*, your child will also get to learn more about history through the true accounts of 8 infamous disasters.

With *Famous Figures of the Early Modern Era*, you'll find that history becomes hands-on as your child assembles movable figures of 10 of the key characters of this time period, from Rembrandt to William Wilberforce.

Photo: The Denoyer Family in Idaho

The Story of the World 3

~~Basic~~ | Complete | Elite

This is very easy to use. Just read aloud 1 chapter from the storybook, then ask your child to tell you what it was about. Afterward, pick an activity page or worksheet that is appropriate for your child's interest and your schedule.

Did you see how big the activity book is? Keep in mind that one of its biggest advantages is the fact that it offers a wide range of activities for each lesson. Pick the ones that best fit your child's learning style and your family's schedule, but don't try to do them all!

One brilliant way to use this text is to approach it from a notebooking perspective. To do this, you'll want to give your child a blank notebook that he will fill with his recap (narration) of each chapter. As he goes on, he'll add art, maps, and even photos of more tangible projects that he does. This is a somewhat labor-intensive approach, but if you're eager for your child to have a firm grasp on world history, it will be hard to beat that method for helping him retain what he learns.

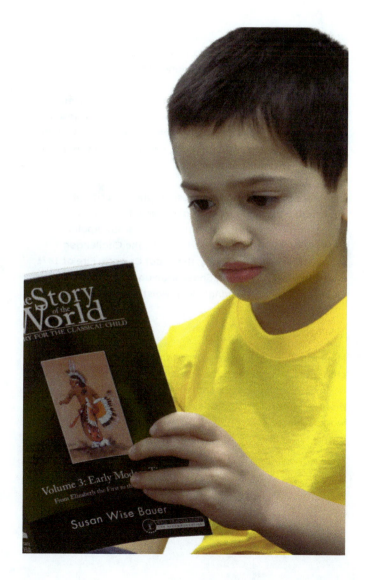

Scheduling

Completing 3 chapters every 2 weeks is a realistic pace that will get you through the books in just under a year.

If you purchased the Elite kit, you'll love having the audiobook download. It includes the same content as the storybook, but it can be much more convenient. Download the files to your device and listen to history with your child while you're driving, cooking, feeding the baby, or any of the myriad other activities that keep your hands too busy to hold a book.

Disasters in History

~~Basic~~ | Complete | Elite

Epic disasters forever transform societies and industries and leave indelible marks in the making of history.

The graphic novel *Disasters in History* includes 8 events that have left their mark on humanity. Some are gruesome accounts that emphasize the brokenness of this world. Others show the resilience of humankind, and some even sparked necessary social change.

Disasters in History makes these gripping stories of important historical disasters accessible to even the most reluctant readers. It includes the events of the Apollo 13 Mission, the Attack on Pearl Harbor, the Challenger Explosion, the Donner Party, the Great Chicago Fire of 1871, the Hindenburg Disaster, Shackleton and the Lost Antarctic Expedition, and the Triangle Shirtwaist Factory Fire.

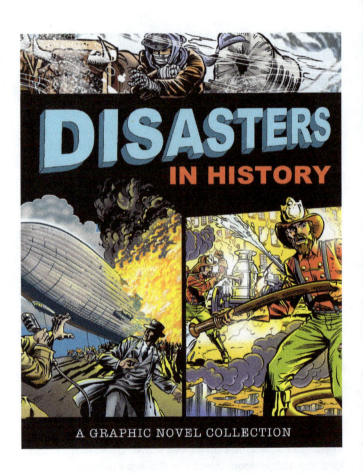

Scheduling

Most families will choose to hand this book over to the student to read at his pace—usually quite fast! You could also assign 1 disaster a week until they are gone, in order to allow more deliberate discussion time. Pick the approach that works best for you.

Famous Figures of the Early Modern Era

~~Basic~~ | ~~Complete~~ | Elite

With *Famous Figures of the Early Modern Era*, you'll find that history becomes hands-on as you assemble movable figures of 21 of the historical people of the early modern era, such as Queen Nzinga, Peter the Great, and Robert Fulton.

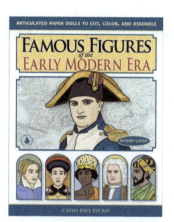

While listening to *The Story of the World*, your avid artist can color in the detailed figures. Using mini brads and a ⅛" hole punch for assembly will allow their arms and legs to move into whatever pose is needed. For the meticulous child who wants it colored exactly right, matching precolored action figures are also included.

Don't forget about the detailed biography section in the front of the book that provides key information about the characters. A companion reading list for each figure is also included, which is perfect if your child wants to learn more or if you're looking for a relevant book for him to read this week.

Scheduling

We suggest completing these figures when you encounter each person in *The Story of the World*. On the following page you'll see the chapters each is mentioned in, or for the few not directly covered in *The Story of the World*, you'll see our ideas of where to slide them in to stay with the time frame / topic of the chapter.

Are you looking for ways to use the completed figures? Your child could put on a puppet show reenacting a historic moment or imagining a more ordinary part of their day. (For added fun, make a video of the performance.)

Use 1 or more of the figures to create a diorama or display representing either the time frame or a particular event.

Do you use a timeline? Add these figures to it!

And, of course, allow your child to engage in creative play with the figures. Sometimes they will capture the imagination in a way that no written text alone will.

Where the figures align with : *The Story of the World 3*:

- Mary, Queen of Scots: chapter 2
- *Rembrandt: chapter 2
- James I of England: chapter 3
- Pocahontas: chapter 3
- Samuel de Champlain: chapter 4
- Queen Nzinga: chapter 7
- Shah Jahan: chapter 11
- Louis XIV: chapter 13
- *Johann Sebastian Bach: chapter 14
- William Penn: chapter 15
- Isaac Newton: chapter 16
- Peter the Great: chapter 17

- Ch'ien-lung: chapter 20
- Captain James Cook: chapter 24
- Catherine the Great: chapter 26
- *Robert Fulton: chapter 27
- Napoleon Bonaparte: chapters 29 and 33
- Sacagawea: chapter 32
- William Clark: chapter 32
- Simón Bolívar: chapter 34
- William Wilberforce: chapter 36

* Signifies this person is not specifically mentioned in *The Story of the World 3* but is pertinent to the named chapter / time frame.

Geography

While *The Story of the World* teaches ancient geography brilliantly, your child will also want to know about the world around him today. The vibrant pages of *Skill Sharpeners Geography* will help him master important geography concepts with a workbook that continually gets rave reviews from families. Puzzleball Globe combines the academic benefits of jigsaw puzzles with the fun of literally putting the world together!

Skill Sharpeners Geography, Grade 3

~~Basic~~ | Complete | Elite

Skill Sharpeners Geography lets your child explore his world while learning key map skills and geography concepts with little fuss on your part. The cross-curricular activities integrate the most current geography standards, and each eye-catching book is divided into colorful collections of engaging, grade-appropriate themes.

Each theme includes short nonfiction reading selections, comprehension questions, vocabulary practice, and writing prompts.

Optional hands-on activities will excite the kinesthetic child in your home. To use them you'll need a few common tools, like scissors, glue, tape, and coloring materials. It may also be helpful to note that there are a couple of activities (pages 69 and 79 in *Skill Sharpeners Geography*) which suggest that you first glue the pieces together and then color the scene. In our opinion, it would at least be worth considering whether to have your child color first and then cut those pieces out. For some kids, that would be less frustrating than coloring on top of glued paper.

Skill Sharpeners Geography takes your child beyond just the basics of geography and includes a smattering of histories and cultures within our world. The colorful illustrations and pages will grab your child's attention, and the handy (removable) answer key in the back allows you to help your student to easily check his work.

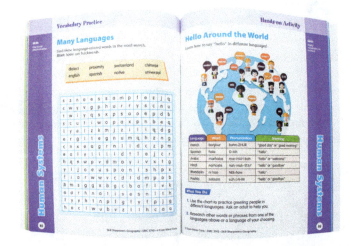

Scheduling

With 132 pages in all this year, complete 4 a week to stay on track. Add in the activities as time and interest allow.

And yes, you may truly skip the activity and writing pages (with no guilt) if that isn't how your child learns best.

Puzzleball Globe

~~Basic~~ | ~~Complete~~ | **Elite**

Puzzles can be educational in so many ways because they stretch your child's brain and improve the way his mind solves problems. While he's solving a puzzle, he's really teaching his brain to work in new ways. As your child solves a geography puzzle, he is mentally drilling himself with physical facts, such as what country goes next to the one he has just completed. Subconsciously, he is making a number of associations as he searches for the next piece.

Flat puzzles of spherical items are easier to assemble, but what if you could hone your geographical skills on something more appropriate, more true to life? Now you can, with the Puzzleball Globe. The Puzzleball Globe can be assembled in 3 different ways. First, use the small number located on each of the curved, nonimage sides of the puzzle piece for easy, systematic assembly. For more of a challenge, use a world map to assemble the globe. Finally, when you think you are ready for the expert level, try assembling the Puzzleball Globe looking only at the puzzle—not your map, the box, or the numbers on the back of each piece.

Decked with animals and landmarks, the Puzzleball Globe consists of 180 beautiful, vibrantly colored, curved, and perfectly crafted puzzle pieces that allow for an exact fit. It is easily assembled with no glue required! A stand is included to display your work of art, but you will have so much fun putting the globe together over and over that you shouldn't be surprised if the stand gets little use!

Scheduling

We suggest having your child complete this once a month until it is too easy for him.

Science

Discover the World

A foundational understanding of scientific principles is critical for students, but if that is delivered in a dreary way, science becomes a drudgery of facts rather than a joyous exploration. This newly launched science series, Discover! Science, aims to inspire a sense of wonder and curiosity towards the natural world in your child.

Discover! Science instills both a passion for discovery and a deep appreciation for scientific exploration.

A Note on Experiments

While conducting every experiment together would be ideal, we understand that your schedule may not always allow for that. If you have a week where you aren't going to be able to complete the experiments, simply discussing the process and expected outcomes can still provide an insightful experience for both you and your child.

Discover! Science

~~Basic~~ | Complete | Elite

Discover! Science is designed from the ground up for the homeschool environment, giving teaching parents added confidence to teach their children with an academically rigorous science curriculum.

Discover! Science combines beautiful student-driven worktexts and parent-friendly instructor guides to offer a science program that encourages multi-modality learning and critical thinking. The colorful pages have easygoing text and a fresh look, focusing on real-world connections to make learning science more appealing for your child.

Discover! Science is designed to develop independent and critical thinking through challenging questions and creative projects. Throughout the worktext, students will learn, reflect, and apply. Concise yet complete instructor guides provide answer keys, additional activities, and challenges, plus ideas for engaging auditory, visual, and kinesthetic learners.

Scheduling

Complete just over 2 lessons a week in this program in order to set a sustainable pace through the school year.

Dr. Bonyfide 1

~~Basic~~ | Complete | Elite

Dr. Bonyfide is a young person's highly entertaining guide to his own body. You know that if your child has basic information about his body, he is more likely to make healthy life choices. Plus, isn't it natural to want to understand why your body works the way it does?

Developed by a team of educators, health professionals, and parents, *Dr. Bonyfide* will creatively guide your child through the bone structures of his body using kid-friendly jokes, rhymes, puzzles, fun facts, and original comic strips. Plus, a pair of X-ray vision (colored) glasses will let your child investigate the bones on special pages. Write-in quizzes and a range of hands-on activities will help you as a teaching parent to assess his progress while simultaneously helping him retain his new knowledge.

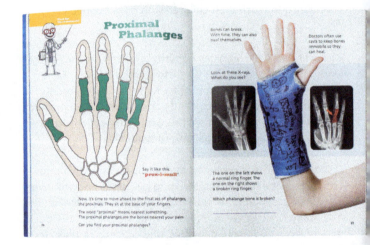

Scheduling

With 108 pages in all, plan on doing 3 a week if you want to make this course last your entire school year. But be prepared—your child may find it so engaging that he races through and finishes it early!

STEM Learning

STEM Is Everywhere!

STEM learning is more than robotics and computer programming. STEM tools also include those that engage students in exploratory learning, discovery, and problem-solving that teach the foundational skills of critical thinking and short- and long-term planning.

So STEM includes your Puzzleball Globe as well as your Smart Dog logic game, even though they are listed in other places in this handbook. Basically anything that goes beyond a rote read-and-regurgitate lesson undoubtedly falls into the STEM classification. In assembling this guide, many of our products could easily have been classified as STEM, but these 2 tools seem especially appropriate for this category.

Photo: The Johanson Family

GraviTrax Academy

~~Basic~~ | Complete | Elite

With GraviTrax Academy, your child can design and build high-tech marble runs while using gravity, magnetism, kinetic energy, momentum, velocity, and problem-solving to propel marbles to the finish.

With this open-ended construction set, your child will have access to 2 types of challenges. In the first, he will be asked to build a marble run precisely as pictured. In the second, he will be told the exact pieces and a few placements, but he will need to complete the design. Both types of instructions have a range of difficulty levels.

We suggest starting with the "precisely as pictured" challenges and then moving to ones he needs to solve. Finally, mix in the volcano add-on for divergent construction challenges.

With over 100 pieces and more than 18 different construction elements, your child will learn how physics impacts the track and his marble. He will experiment with how height, curves, free-fall, and even a magnetic cannon can control the speed of the marble. GraviTrax Deluxe combines physics, architecture, and engineering and will sharpen your child's spatial reasoning, logical planning, and architectural design skills.

Photo: The Liwanag Family in Chester, New York

GraviTrax The Game: Impact

The game portion of GraviTrax takes all the fun of GraviTrax and makes it into a logic puzzle. GraviTrax the Game: Impact has 30 building tasks to solve with increasing levels of difficulty. All the pieces you need to complete these new challenges are included and are compatible with all other GraviTrax building sets.

The front of each task card provides a game set-up and shows the pieces required to solve the challenge. Next, add the tiles, rails, and hammer to create a path for the marble to reach the landing tile. Think you've got it? Test it by launching the marble. If needed, rework your design and try again! If you get stuck, tasks 1-29 each have a hint on the back of the task card, and tasks 1-28 have a solution in the booklet. For tasks 29 and 30, it is up to the GraviTrax community to discover the answer!

See our quick start guide on the next page to get up and running fast.

Scheduling

GraviTrax Deluxe with the volcano add-on includes 33 models to build, plus as many as your child improvises. We suggest 1 per week, starting with the exact replication manual.

GraviTrax The Game: Impact has 30 challenges to solve. We suggest also completing 1 of these per week.

That brings you to a total of 2 GraviTrax Academy challenges for each week to complete the course within your school year!

How to Play GraviTrax the Game: Impact

For pictorial instructions, you can visit the manufacturer's website at https://www.ravensburger.us/start/gravitrax-the-game-tutorial/index.html#Impact

Are you ready to play the game but don't know where to start? Place the tutorial cards in front of you. These are the 6 cards with the green border.

Step 1 - Prepare to Play

Look at the first Task Card, Task Card 0. Place the base plate you need in front of you and position it in the right direction. If there are several base plates on the card, build them together as shown on the Task Card. Now, place the building elements shown in the overview in front of you and all the parts you don't need to one side.

Step 2 - Set-up

Put the Starter and the Finish tile on the same squares as shown on the Task Card. Check to see if height tiles are needed underneath the Starter and Finish.

Hint: Use the green squares of the base plate as a guide to position the tiles.

Step 3 - Position

When placing the Starter and Finish tiles, ensure that the tiles' entrances and exits match the Task Card. Also, ensure that you put the marble on the right exit of the Starter tile.

Step 4 - Challenge

Think about how you can build a track from Start to Finish. Use the contents you have put to one side and see if you can solve the challenge.

Important: You can and must use only the building elements shown on the Task Card, and all must be used.

Tip: You can find hints to solve the challenge on the back of the Task Cards.

Step 5: Check

Do you think you have solved the challenge? Release the marble to test the track. If the marble reaches the Finish tile, you have solved the puzzle.

The instruction booklet depicts all the solutions for Tasks 1-28. Once you have solved the challenge, you can check your track with the solutions in the instruction booklet. For Tasks 29 and 30, we will leave it up to you and the GraviTraxer community to find the answer. You can share your solution under #GraviTraxTHEGAME30.

Have fun solving the mysteries!

Typing Instructor for Kids

~~Basic~~ | Complete | Elite

Using proven typing techniques, children will master the keyboard while journeying with Toby and Lafitte to 5 imaginary lands where they learn proper typing techniques and build keyboarding skills. Just choose a typing plan and set a words-per-minute goal. As your child explores Typer Island, he will learn typing along the way.

The engaging lessons and exercises teach children important typing skills, including speed and accuracy. If your child finds your old typing program boring, and if you are looking for the right balance of education, entertainment, and motivation in a typing program, then you will appreciate this course.

Typing Instructor for Kids offers 30-plus action-packed, multilevel game challenges; graduated drills and lesson plans; hundreds of activities, exercises, and tests; and bilingual learning in English and Spanish.

Scheduling

The only limit is your schedule, but we suggest 3 lessons a week.

Emotional Intelligence

Social Skills and More

Emotional literacy is as necessary as learning the ABCs. If your child is unable to identify and manage his own emotions, or if he doesn't understand others' emotions, then successful relationships will be difficult.

On a day-to-day level, studies show that cultivating your child's social-emotional skills can result in less aggression and anxiety and teach better social problem–solving skills. That's worth a lot, isn't it?

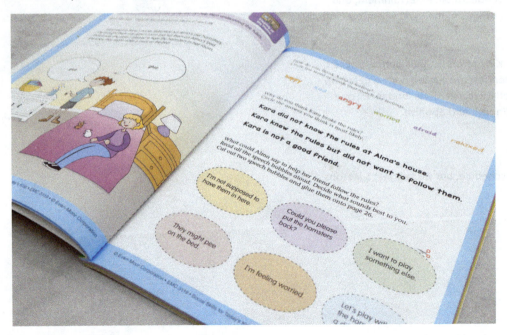

Social Skills Activities for Today's Kids

~~Basic~~ | ~~Complete~~ | <mark>Elite</mark>

When discussing homeschooling, people often raise the inevitable question about socialization. Fortunately, homeschoolers have opportunities to develop these skills through planned social activities, group projects, and extracurricular activities. Yet regardless of a child's academic path, there's value in systematically practicing and preparing for social situations in their everyday lives. That's where *Social Skills Activities for Today's Kids* comes in.

These colorful workbooks offer engaging activities designed to help children practice and prepare for various social scenarios they encounter—making friends, navigating group settings, going out in public, or interacting online.

Social Skills Activities reinforces basic social skills and provides a platform for parents to guide their children in aligning with family preferences and boundaries. With the help of *Social Skills Activities for Today's Kids*, children can confidently navigate the complexities of social interaction and thrive in various settings.

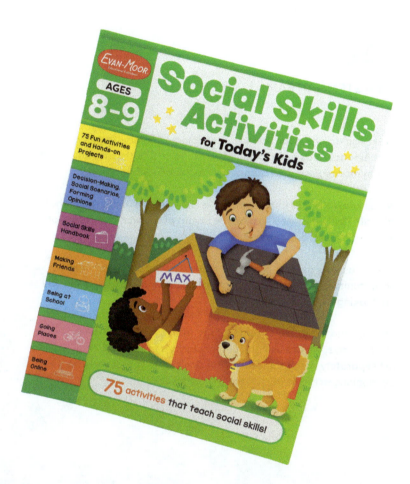

Scheduling

Social Skills Activities includes 75 activities including topics such as lunchtime behavior or talking to a friend's parents. We recommend completing 2-3 activities a week. If the activities are more than a page or 2 long, just complete 2 activities. If they are short ones, then go ahead and add a third so that you will finish the book by the end of 36 weeks.

Art

Art + STEM = STEAM

STEM—an acronym for Science, Technology, Engineering, and Mathematics—has been joined by Art to form STEAM, and now the 2 acronyms are used interchangeably in the academic world.

We all know STEM is important, but is the addition of art really that critical? Yes! Art is used to plan the layout of a tower, the design of a prosthetic hand, and the colors of the latest app.

In fact, as long as your project is inquiry-based and you have the opportunity to think critically, creatively, and innovatively, then you are looking at a STEAM curriculum.

Because the transition of terminology from STEM to STEAM is still tentative, we are using STEM for clarity's sake and listing art separately in this handbook. But don't let that fool you into overlooking art this year. It really is a vital skill!

Paint-by-Number Museum Series

~~Basic~~ | Complete | Elite

With the Paint-by-Number Museum Series, your young artist will get to imitate 4 very different famous masterpieces: *The Eiffel Tower* by Georges Seurat, *Irises* and *Sunflowers*—both by Vincent van Gogh, and *The Japanese Footbridge* by Claude Monet.

Painting by number is often seen as being simplistic, uninspired, and mechanical. Yet Leonardo da Vinci himself assigned assistants to paint in numbered areas on a work that he had already sketched out. Completing paint-by-number projects helps your child learn to analyze a subject and observe areas of color, and it is an excellent exercise in brush control and strokes as he focuses entirely on getting the right color in the right spot.

Unlike other paint-by-number sets, the Paint-by-Number Museum Series does not print the numbers on each canvas but rather on reference sheets so your artist can choose to imitate the masterpiece or paint with his own matchless style. Brief illustrated instructions with a snippet about the techniques used by the master artists when creating their works of art will get your miniaturist to the easel fast. The attention to detail and the skills developed are sure to set in motion a lifetime of art appreciation.

Scheduling

With 4 paintings to complete, you could set these aside for special occasions or otherwise dreary weeks. Or choose to allow your child to work on them a little bit every day until he has finished them!

The Nature Explorer's Drawing Guide

~~Basic~~ | Complete | Elite

Fuel your child's curiosity and ignite creativity with *The Nature Explorer's Drawing Guide for Kids*!

This valuable guidebook, tailored for budding explorers and aspiring artists, is brimming with step-by-step drawing lessons and fascinating facts about the natural world. With each turn of the page, your child will embark on an exciting journey of discovery, learning how to capture the beauty of animals, trees, flowers, and more through art.

The author provides simple yet engaging lessons, along with handy tips and tricks, to inspire your child to venture outdoors and observe the wonders of nature firsthand. With over 40 subjects to draw and learn about, *The Nature Explorer's Drawing Guide for Kids* offers endless opportunities for creative expression and learning.

(Scheduling)

We suggest 1 sketch a week. Occasionally add in a second sketch, and your child will complete all 40 sketches within 36 weeks.

Have I Got a Story for You!

~~Basic~~ | ~~Complete~~ | <mark>Elite</mark>

Have I Got a Story for You! is a one-of-a-kind multi-child art history course that is part story, part adventure, part art studio, and 100% fun! Used for 13 years at a prominent college preparatory school, this course is now available to you via high-quality videos.

This year your student will study the Baroque period. He will be introduced to various artists, hear about cultural events specific to that era, and examine masterpieces for style or techniques that make them unique. An animated cartooned drop of paint named Gasfy adds an element of lightheartedness to each episode's journey.

Have I Got a Story for You! consists of twelve 20-30-minute videos with corresponding lesson plans. Throughout each series, 3 artists are introduced. Students will analyze the masterpieces of these prominent artists and discuss how their culture, circumstances, and family influenced their art and more. And for those who blush at nudity in art, *Have I Got a Story for You!* is entirely G-rated. This means all nudity has been pixelated out—quite a feat!

Corresponding to each video are detailed lesson plans that include critical thinking questions to engage your students in discussion and generate higher-order thinking skills. The lesson plans also suggest optional cross-curricular age-specific activities in the areas of writing and vocabulary. As a bonus, some lesson plans include geography, history, and even science assignments.

But what your children will love most are the well-chosen art activities. Several are suggested for each unit, each selected

to enhance your child's retention of the lecture material. Most art activities will take about 30 minutes to complete.

Scheduling

Complete 1 lesson every 3 weeks. If you want to invest the same amount of time each week, it will likely work best to watch the video on week 1 and then complete some of the related art projects on weeks 2 and 3. Others of you may wish to watch the series 3 times over the year (Some third-graders love repetition!), in which case we'd suggest watching a video lesson and doing 1 of the art projects each week.

Our family is using this course for "cousin school," and it works well to have the entire crew watch the video first and then roll right into a related art project.

There is no "right" way to implement this—play with it and see what works best for your family!

Learning Tools

Learning Styles and More

Do you know your child's learning style? If not, take a few moments to research it. (Most researchers note at least 3: hands-on or kinesthetic learners, auditory learners, and visual learners. Many children are a unique combination of these.)

If you don't know which methods equip your child to learn best, you will want to take a few moments to research them. Once you know your child's strengths and weaknesses, you'll be able to focus on methods that help him learn rather than using the approach you've always used. (All students find it helpful to integrate as many learning modes as possible into their studies.)

For instance, if you find you have a kinesthetic learner, encourage him to move while he learns. Break out the Needoh Cube, let him sign keywords to himself, or write them on a whiteboard.

If he's an auditory learner, make it a point to have him hear the information he's learning. You could read it to him, encourage him to read aloud, use an audio version, or download a podcast. However you decide to approach it will be better than reading the same textbook silently 4 dozen times.

By the way, visual learners will probably have the easiest time learning. Most information is naturally presented visually in textbooks.

visual

auditory

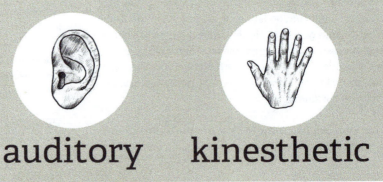

kinesthetic

Test Prep: Grade 3

~~Basic~~ | Complete | Elite

Home-taught children who are not prepared for their yearly standardized tests are at a distinct disadvantage to government- and privately-taught children. If you reside in a state that requires standardized tests, you should know that a vast majority of certified teachers teach with the test in mind. In other words, teachers understand the types of questions that will appear on the standardized tests, and they will spend weeks preceding the tests covering the necessary information. If you do not do likewise, your children stand a chance of performing poorly in comparison.

For those of us in a state where some form of testing is required but never scrutinized, preparing is not as critical. But some of you are in states where the test results are not only analyzed but are also used as a basis for whether you may continue to home educate. Why not make sure your children are on a level playing field? The Test Prep series offers students the essential groundwork needed to prepare for standardized tests.

Based on subject areas covered by most state standardized tests, these colorful, inviting workbooks provide a good sampling of all the skills required of each grade level. Practice pages, strategies, tips, and full-length practice tests build test-taking confidence and skills in subjects such as reading comprehension, vocabulary, language, and math. The test tips are beneficial, and the information and instructions are super-easy to follow. Developed by a leading educational publisher, Harcourt's *Test Prep* provides a great opportunity for children to review before taking standardized state tests. Engaging, practical, and easy to use, *Test Prep* will help your children face the tests with the same confidence that their peers will have.

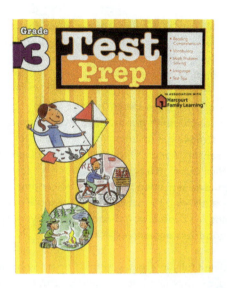

Even if your state doesn't require testing, consider completing the book anyway since test-taking skills are vital across all areas of life

Scheduling

Our family has always preferred to spend the week or 2 before our state-mandated annual testing working through this book. Keep it low-key, and let the change of pace be an enjoyable experience for your child. If you run into a concept he doesn't know, stop and explain it to him; that is why you are doing the prep now!

NeeDoh Nice Cube

~~Basic~~ | ~~Complete~~ | <mark>Elite</mark>

The NeeDoh Nice Cube is a tactile sensation that offers this unique experience: it's soft when slowly squished and dense when quickly squished, always returning to its original shape to provide endless tactile fun.

Each NeeDoh Nice Cube starts firm but quickly softens as it warms in your student's hands. Once it cools down, it regains its firmness, making it an ideal hand exerciser for fine motor skills and sensory needs. With its satisfying weight, the NeeDoh Nice Cube offers the perfect tactile experience. But this squishy sensation isn't just visually appealing; it's incredibly satisfying to touch. It's like having a giant, squishy, non-melting ice cube at your fingertips, ready to deliver stretchy goodness and endless fun.

Your child can fully interact with this fidget toy by pulling, squeezing, or smushing it to his heart's content. As he engages with the NeeDoh Nice Cube, he'll experience a delightful sensory sensation that aids in calming restless hands and enhancing focus and attention.

More About NeeDoh

While learning new things is always exciting as your child works to get his head around a new concept, general anxiety is also a common experience. NeeDoh, is the ultimate stress reliever that will help your student become calm. Its tactile surface and soft yet solid interior provide endless enjoyment. NeeDoh is known for its durable squish that allows your child to relax and regain composure. Parents of neurodivergent children, those with ADHD, OCD, autism, anxiety, and more, will find that NeeDoh helps children focus and pay attention with each squeeze.

Each NeeDoh is filled with a non-toxic, dough-like compound created from a PVA glue compound, making it safe for kids. Even after a session of rugged squeezing, each figure always returns to its original shape. It's small enough to fit in the palm of your hand, making it the perfect companion for those moments when you need to decompress.

A simple wash with soap and warm water, followed by air drying, will keep it in tip-top condition. Please note that colors may vary, but relaxation and fun are guaranteed.

Scheduling

Plan to keep your child's NeeDoh Nice Cube handy during his lessons. NeeDoh Nice Cube is perfect for playing with while he watches his math lessons or at other times when his mind is more engaged than his hands.

Grip Colored EcoPencils

~~Basic~~ | ~~Complete~~ | Elite

Whether for artwork or schoolwork, Faber-Castell's Grip Colored EcoPencils are a good fit for elementary students. The Grip Colored EcoPencils feature an ergonomic triangular barrel and a patented grip zone for fatigue-free, comfortable drawing. Not only that, but the triangular design of these pencils also helps prevent rollaways.

Artists will enjoy having 24 colors to incorporate into their pictures, while students will appreciate the selection for color-specific workbook assignments. The rich pigmentation of the core makes the Grip Colored EcoPencils' colors vibrant. What a great set of pencils to equip your young artist!

Schedule

No need to schedule these pencils. Just pull them out whenever your child's worksheets or art projects would benefit!

Articles and Resources

From Our Family to Yours

39 Years of Serving You

In 1985, we were a family of 5. I was the oldest of 3 toddler girls with a mom who absolutely excelled at educating us at home. This was during the "Dark Ages" of homeschooling, and online searching was still a thing of the future. Our mom, Deb, was (and is) a voracious reader and an avid researcher. We girls were thriving academically, and other moms were naturally interested in using the same curricula Deb had found.

That same year, she and Dan, our dad, repurposed the business license originally intended for their world-class Golden Retriever breeding operation, which had come to naught, and she launched Timberdoodle, a homeschool supply company. She created our first catalog, and growth came fast. We shipped curriculum from our laundry room, our grandparents' basement, and finally warehouses and an office. Two more children were added to the family, and we all grew up working in the business from an early age.

Now, decades later, Timberdoodle is still renowned for out-of-the-box learning and crazy-smart finds. Mom's engineering background has heavily influenced our STEM selections and warehouse layout, and her no-nonsense, independent approach has made these kits the award-winning choice that they are today.

All 5 of us children are grown now, and most still work at Timberdoodle in key roles. Our brother and his wife have welcomed 4 amazing little ones in the past 7 years, and we sisters have opened our home to children through foster care

and adoption. As our families have grown, we've become even more committed to equipping parents with the best homeschooling resources. The kits we sell are the same ones we use in our own homes, and we hope you enjoy them as much as we do.

In the following articles, you'll hear Deb and others talk about some of the nitty-gritty questions we receive. Do you have a question not answered here? You are invited to contact us at any time—we'd love to help!

Joy (for all of us)

Picture circa 1989, breaking ground for our first warehouse!

Why Emphasize Independent Learning?

The Top 7 Reasons This Is Such a Big Deal at Timberdoodle

1. Avoid Burnout

One-on-one teaching is critical to the success of any student, and homeschoolers are no exception to that. However, we have seen parents become helicopter teachers, micromanaging every detail of their students' education. Is it any wonder that these parents burn out? Independent learning skills provide a natural transition from the one-on-one focus of early childhood to a less teacher-intense educational approach.

2. Cultivate Responsible Learners

There is a lot of (Dare we say it?) fun in teaching. But it is better for your students if they master how to learn on their own. After all, when they are adults, you'll want them to have the ability to pick up any skill they want and learn it as needed. Structuring their education to be more and more self-taught helps them to become responsible independent learners.

3. Special Needs, Illness, and Newborns

Not all parents have the same amount of teaching time. Whether they are doing therapy for a child with special needs, dealing with a chronic illness, managing visits for a foster child, or are blessed with a newborn, there are seasons when homeschooling needs to be more independent for the teacher's sanity!

Photo: The Elie Family in California

4. You Don't Have to Love Teaching

As much as no one wants to mention this, we all know parents who struggle to teach. They love their kids and feel strongly about homeschooling, but when it actually comes down to teaching, they are easily overwhelmed and intimidated. If it is an area they are not gifted or trained in, then of course teaching is scary. Independent learning tools can help parent educators get comfortable in their role. Even if they never love teaching, they can still reap the benefits of giving their children a superior education at home.

5. Timberdoodle's Purpose: We Are Here to Make Giving Your Children a Superior Education at Home Enjoyable

Here at Timberdoodle, amid the catalogs, sales, blog posts, videos, Facebook giveaways, etc., we have one primary goal. That goal is to make it possible for parents to enjoy giving their children a superior education at home. We aren't here just to sell you stuff (though we wouldn't exist if you didn't shop!), which is why we have been known to send you to our "competitors" when their product would work better for you. We really just want you to be a happy homeschool family. When that happens, we feel successful! Independent learning is one tool in your toolbox. It is a valuable tool, so use it where it works best for you.

6. Not Either/Or

You don't have to pick between independent and group learning across the board. History and science are typically easy subjects to combine across multiple grades as it is wonderful to have the whole family involved in the read-aloud portion and experiments. Our family has also converted some workbooks into read-alouds. Instead of writing in answers, we took turns answering the questions. If you're seeing that one of your texts this year would benefit the entire family, why not switch it up a little? Just because you want your children to master independent learning, that does not mean you should hesitate to learn as a family!

7. Our Family's Experience

The rule of thumb in our house was that as soon as a child could read, he was responsible for his own education. We each had an annual conference with Mom to set learning goals for the year. We were then given the books for the year—often including the teacher's manuals. Mom gave us each a weekly checklist to complete before Friday Family Night. If we needed help, we asked questions. Otherwise, the responsibility was ours. This also freed us up to do other important things as a family: service, Timberdoodle work, babysitting, elder care, community or church projects, hospitality, farming…

What Makes Games a Priority?

6 Reasons Games Aren't Just for Fun—Even the "Frivolous" Games

You may have noticed there is at least 1 multiplayer game in every Timberdoodle curriculum kit. This is not just to add some levity to your day!

The Research

A quick Google search will net you numerous articles on the benefits of playing board games with your children:

- increasing laughter
- language development
- understanding rules
- grasping fair play
- detecting patterns and predicting outcomes
- learning from experience
- impulse control
- social skills
- increasing focus
- teamwork
- reducing anxiety
- unplugging from technology
- increasing analytical abilities
- setting goals
- patience
- problem-solving skills
- reducing stress
- creativity
- prioritizing steps toward a goal
- self-confidence
- spatial ability

This is a robust and interwoven list, but here are the 6 things that have jumped out at us over the past years and made games a huge priority for education.

1. Social-Emotional Intelligence

Think of your closest and dearest friends outside of your immediate family. What makes them so dear to you? My guess is that it isn't their IQ or ability to speed-solve a complex math problem. A friendship will celebrate those interesting facts, but your friendship itself is more likely rooted in shared interests, time spent together, and an ability to navigate hard situations with grace.

When you spend time teaching a child how to lose graciously, you are teaching a life skill that will translate into all of life and impact his friendships way more than his test scores ever could.

In light of this, the end of each game may be more important than the strategy in the middle. Coach your children in what you expect from the winner and the loser. Around here, a "Good game!" goes a long way, but you decide what is best for your family. Humility is what you're looking for—not the teary deflation of a proud loser or the puffed-up bragging of a proud winner!

2. Strategic Thinking

Obviously, the games we've chosen require age-appropriate logic and strategy. Critical thinking skills are essential, so let's teach them any way we can.

3. Connection

Sometimes it can seem that you spend more time correcting your children's behavior than connecting with them. Then as they grow older, your parenting becomes more and more hands-off. Making games a priority at all ages lets you enjoy each other's company and genuinely become closer to each other. What parent won't appreciate that?

4. Executive Functioning

Are you familiar with executive functioning? It is the ability to prioritize and organize information. The clearest example is the age-old challenge to "guess what number I'm thinking of right now using yes-or-no questions." If you respond by asking if the number is higher than 100, you are using executive functioning. If instead you start rattling off specific numbers, you're not. In games, you're constantly taking into consideration what your opponent is doing, what pieces are still in your hand, which rules apply at the moment while sorting and utilizing all the information to decide what your next game play should be.

5. Regulation

Some articles tie this to executive functioning, but it's worth discussing on its own. Regulation is the ability to control your own emotions. Can you think of a more natural opportunity to practice this than during game play? Calm-down strategies and redos may be implemented as many times as needed until your child is able to endure suspense and even win or lose without outbursts. Whew!

6. Growth Mindset

Some of us, students included, tend to think that either we are good at something or we're not. When our twins were young, this was particularly obvious in our discussions about art. One had a natural inclination for drawing, but one did

not. So the naturally gifted one called himself an artist and proclaimed that his brother was not. It was helpful to come back and discuss that we all learn and grow. So when Mr. Artist set aside his art for several months and his twin worked and worked at it, we had 2 artists on our hands! Game play is a natural place to model that all of us learn and grow. We aren't "born with it," but we learn skills and develop abilities.

Side Note: Think Out Loud

An article from Parenting Science made the excellent point that students don't always naturally ask why a player used a specific strategy. Try to start that conversation by asking why he chose that specific move or explaining that you're starting with this piece because (insert strategy here). This will model the higher-order thinking that you are setting out to teach. It will also model the fact that we are all learners!

So what are you waiting for? Go play some games!

7 Reasons to Stop Schoolwork and Go Build Something!

Photo: The Denoyer Family in Idaho

Would you like to supplement your curriculum with a program that simultaneously improves your child's visual perception, patience, problem-solving, spatial perception, creativity, ability to follow directions, grasp of physics concepts, and engineering ability? Better yet, what if your child would actually enjoy this curriculum and choose to do it whenever he could?

No, this isn't some mythical homeschool product guaranteed to solve all your problems for a large fee—we are talking about the Lego bricks already strewn throughout your house, the blocks in our preschool curriculum, and the Bioloid robot kit designed for teens.

Construction kits just might be the most underrated type of curriculum ever. It's not just us; research concludes that children learn a lot by designing and building things. Based on our own engineering background, we believe that construction is one of the most valuable educational processes available and that both learning to build and learning by what has been built should be a part of every family's curriculum. Here are our top 7 skills your child will learn with his construction kit.

1. Visual Perception

It may be obvious that it takes visual perception to find the right pieces and place them well, but consider that whether your child is reading, finishing a puzzle, or doing open-heart surgery, proficiency in visual perception is mandatory.

2. Patience

Do you know anyone who couldn't stand to be a little more patient? Construction takes time. Slowing down, reading the directions, doing it over when a piece has been placed wrong or a sibling knocks over your creation...these are all valuable character-building experiences.

3. Problem-Solving

Some children lack the ability to troubleshoot a situation and figure out the next step. Construction sets provide a structured opportunity to figure out what went wrong and fix it, if you're following the directions. If you are designing your own models, you'll have even more opportunities to solve problems.

4. Spatial Perception

Probably the clearest picture of how important it is to be able to mentally convert 2D images into 3D objects is that of a surgeon. Knowing where the spleen is on a 2D textbook page isn't nearly the same thing as being able to reach into an incision and find the damaged organ.

5. Creativity

Not every creative person has artistic ability. But construction can open the doors of creativity like no other tool. What if I move this gear over here? Could I build that bridge with only blue pieces?

6. Following Directions

Some children are natural rule followers and need to be encouraged to be creative. Others need contraint to follow directions, at least on occasion. If your child falls into that camp, construction kits are a natural way to encourage him in this skill, with the added benefit of a finished result he can show off.

7. Grasp of Physics

Friction, force, mass, and energy are all basic physics concepts much more easily explained and grasped with a set of blocks and a ball than by studying a dry textbook definition.

What If This Is Too Hard?

9 Steps to Take If You're Feeling Overwhelmed

Photo: The Porters in Alaska

Everyone has felt overwhelmed at some point in his education. Whether it's a groan from you as you pull a giant textbook out of the box or the despair from your child when he's read the directions 5 times and the STEM model *still* isn't operating as he wants it to, you will almost certainly hit a moment this year when you realize that an aspect of homeschooling is harder than you anticipated.

So what do you do now?

1. Take a Breath

Just knowing that everyone faces this should help you relax a bit. This feeling will not last—you'll get through this!

2. Jump In!

Ask yourself why you are stressed right now. Is it because something is so intimidating that you have been avoiding it? If that's the case, the simplest solution is to jump in and get started. Could you read just the first page together before lunch? What if you have your student find all of the pieces for step 1 today? Sometimes it's better to muddle through a lesson together than to wait until you're ready to teach it perfectly.

3. Step Back

Perhaps you're too close right now. If you're midproject and totally frustrated by how it's going, try the opposite approach. Close the book for 30 minutes (Set a timer!) and go grab lunch, hit the playground, or swap to a more hands-on project. When the timer rings, you and your student will be ready to try again with clearer heads.

4. Time This

Timers are an invaluable learning tool. If you're becoming distracted, try setting a 10- or 20-minute timer during which you'll do only one thing. Or tell yourself you definitely need to tackle That Dreaded Subject, but only for 30 minutes a day in two 15-minute chunks. When the timer rings, close the text and move to the next thing. Dividing your day into blocks of time can make a remarkable difference in your efficiency level.

5. Level Down

Did your student take the math pretest before jumping in this year? If not, perhaps he is just in the wrong level! If moving to an easier level freaks you out, it may help to remember that you and your student are not defined by his skill set in any field. Faking his way through by blood, sweat, and tears does not help his future self. Taking the time to back up and fill in the gaps, though, will benefit him forever!

6. Simplify

If you are trying to do every possible activity in every course, it's no wonder you're exhausted. By the time your student is in high school, he will need to complete 75% or more of the work in each course to get full credits. We're not advocates of doing the work in name only, but it's OK to watch some experiments online rather than completing each one yourself. It's also appropriate to do only every other math problem in a section if your child is bored to tears with yet another page of addition. Doesn't that feel better?

7. Make Accommodations

What exactly is stressing your student (or you!) out right now? Is it the pen-to-paper writing component? Why not let him use the computer and type his work instead? Or perhaps he can dictate to you and you write for him. Make sure you're doing whatever you can to engage his best learning style.

Encourage Mr. Auditory Learner to read aloud. Or break out all of the favorite fidgets and let Miss Kinesthetic work at a standing desk.

8. Ask for Help

Ask another teacher/parent to work through the issue with you. You may be surprised by how much clarity you gain with a fresh perspective. (Our Facebook groups can be great for this!)

9. Get Professional Help

Check the publisher's website, the book's teacher page, or the kit's manual for contact information. Most of the authors and manufacturers we work with are fantastic about helping and coaching those who get stuck. Not getting the help you need from them? Contact mail@Timberdoodle.com or call us at 800-478-0672, and we'll work with them to get that answer for you.

9 Tips for Homeschooling Gifted Children

From a Family Who Knows This Journey

1. Disdain Busywork

Your child wants to learn, so don't slow him down! If he has mastered multiplication, why are you still spending an hour a day reviewing it? Yes, he does need some review, but we've seen way too many families focus on completing every problem rather than mastering the material. One way to test this is to have him complete every other review problem on only the most essential pages and see how he does. If he can prove he knows it, he doesn't need to be spending quite as much time there.

2. Go Deep

Allow breathing room in your schedule so you have time to investigate earth's gravitational pull or the advantages and disadvantages of hair sheep vs. woolly sheep. Remember that your child is asking to learn, so why pull him away from the subject that's fascinating him? After all, we know that material we're interested in sticks with us so much better than things we learn only because we must.

3. Go Fast

If your child wants to take 3 science courses this year or race through 2 math levels, then why not let him? Homeschoolers can absolutely rock this because there is no one holding us to a "traditional" pace!

4. Encourage Completion

Sometimes it seems there is a touch of ADD in every genius. Give your child as much flexibility as you possibly can, but also keep in mind that you'll be doing him a disservice if he never has to complete something he doesn't feel like working on. Sometimes he may even be surprised to realize that the very subject he dreaded is the springboard for a whole new area of investigation!

5. Give Space and Opportunities

If you can keep mandatory studies to a minimum, you'll give your child more opportunities to accelerate his learning in the areas where he is gifted. Common sense, perhaps, but also worth deliberately thinking through as you plan your school year.

6. Work on Weak Areas Carefully

While you definitely want to help your student overcome his struggles, you also want to be careful that a weakness in one area doesn't impede his progress in other ways. For instance, a child may struggle with writing because his brain works much faster than his hands. While we still encourage working on handwriting skills, we also suggest that his parents try teaching him to type and allow him to complete writing assignments on the computer. This lets him continue to build his writing skills instead of holding him back because of his lack of handwriting speed.

7. Emphasize Humility and Service

We have met way too many children who are obnoxiously convinced that they are geniuses and that everyone needs to be in awe of their abilities. Your child will be much healthier (and happier!) if he realizes these 4 things:

- His identity is *never* found in his brainpower.
- Even as gifted as he is, there are still things that others do better than he does.
- Don't weigh him down by constantly telling him how big his brain is. He is much more than his brain. (Should he lose his edge, he won't lose his worth!)
- His gifts are not for himself alone but for serving others.

Of course, the goal is not to shame, insult, or degrade him but to give him a framework from which he can truly thrive and be free to learn. With a proper perspective, he'll be able to enjoy learning without the burden of constantly assessing his genius and worrying what people think of him.

Encourage his learning, but don't forget to cultivate his character. In 10 years, his response to rebuke will be much more telling than his test score this year, so don't put an inordinate amount of stress on intellectual pursuits.

8. Talk—a LOT!

Talk about what he's interested in. Talk about the theories he came up with today. Talk about his daydreams. Talk about what he wants to study next. Talk about why he may actually need to master that most-dreadful-of-subjects, whatever that may be. Not only will you be able to impart your years of wisdom to him, but you'll also know well the subjects he's interested in so you can link those to his other studies, the places you're visiting next week, or that interesting article you read yesterday.

9. Relax!

Your child is a wonderful gift, but don't feel the need to maximize his potential at every moment. As a side benefit, just relaxing about his genius may in fact increase it. Our own family found that some of our best test scores came after a year off of most formal schooling. Not what we would have planned, but a very valuable insight. Living life also equals learning, so maximize that!

Photo: The Siyow Family in Florida

11 Thoughts for Homeschooling Struggling Children

From a Family Who Knows This Journey Too!

If you were to call me up and ask for help with a struggling child, these are some of the questions I might toss your way as our conversation got underway.

What Do You Mean by "Struggling"?

If you tell me that your child stomps his foot and walks away when you mention it's almost school time, I will have a different answer than I will for the child who cries because his math is too complex or the 10-year-old who cannot seem to grasp phonics. Each child is struggling, but the answers must vary! So as you go through my questions here, please disregard any that don't apply and always feel free to reach out to us with a more specific question.

1. Investigate Root Issues

Is every visual task a challenge? Consider a thorough eye and tracking exam. Perhaps phonics are a struggle. How's his hearing? We've had sad, grumpy children respond to addressing underlying health issues like undiagnosed stomach pain, untreated sleep challenges, or vitamin deficiencies. (Don't worry. We aren't about to start preaching certain supplements—but if the idea to consider things like this has never occurred to you, our story may be helpful!) We've also had children whose anxiety or ADHD made it incredibly hard to focus. Knowing *why* something is a struggle may open up new ideas for solving the problem.

2. Embrace Repetition

Does doing more reps solve the problem? If your child finds that a single page of math isn't enough to cement the concept, what if you assign 2 pages? Or if reading is the issue, could you go back to square one with a different program and get a different result?

3. Check His Memory

If you ask him to repeat back random letters or digits, how many can he accurately imitate (e.g., "7, A, Y, 2")? Do this orally to check auditory memory / processing and visually to assess his visual processing / memory.

You generally want to see 7 digits or more in ages 7+. Any less than that and you may have found a huge clue to what skill to work on!

4. Back Up

While you could continue with math work that is on-grade and explain each component over and over, it is highly likely that your student will advance much faster if he starts over with the basics and races through. And he'll do that with less strain on your relationship and less stress for either of you. The same applies to many subjects, particularly if you were not the one who was teaching him when he was at a previous level or if you now know that the old program wasn't using the approach best suited for him.

5. Check Engagement

Is it possible that this is a motivational issue? Even if that is not the primary issue, motivation may help. We have some children who struggle academically due to early life trauma. Rather than throwing up our hands, it has been very helpful to realize that yes, he will work harder at this than his peers might, so he may also need a bigger carrot than his peers. If you pull out all the stops for a week, does that help at all?

6. Really Invest in His Learning Style

How does your child learn best? If he needs auditory repetition, can you record the lesson for him to play back or choose an audio-based course? Or if he's hands-on, make sure you pull out the manipulatives every time for now. Not sure? Take some time to study the skills he has mastered and how he learned them.

7. Make Accommodations

Just as you might do for your gifted child, you want to be careful that a weakness in one area doesn't impede his progress in other ways. For instance, a child may struggle with writing because his brain works much faster than his hands. While we still encourage such a child to work on handwriting skills, we will probably also get him started on typing (TTRS can be very helpful!) and allow him to complete writing assignments on the computer. This lets him continue to build his writing skills instead of holding him back because of his lack of handwriting speed.

For your ADHD child, this may look like installing a trampoline in your dining room and encouraging short breaks to calm his system. What might make this better for him? How do you get there?

8. Timers

We are an ADHD-type household, and one huge impact this has is in time management. Rather than stress over lost time, a visual timer has helped us all. Your student can race

the timer, enjoy a special privilege if he beats the timer, or receive practice work if he is opting to daydream instead of working.

9. Emphasize Humility and Service

Just like your gifted child, your struggling child will be much healthier (and happier!) if he realizes these 3 things:
- His identity is *never* found in his brainpower.
- He is indeed gifted in some areas. (Help him find these!)
- His gifts are not for himself alone but for serving others, and he is excellent at that.

Encourage his learning, but don't forget to cultivate his character. In 10 years, his response to rebuke will be much more telling than his test score this year, so don't put an inordinate amount of stress on intellectual pursuits.

10. Tutors

You aren't abdicating your role as a teacher if you realize that separating parenting from math would be helpful for your teen right now!

11. Relax!

When your child is an adult out in the real world, it really won't matter if he learned to read at age 2 or 12. Yes, you want to make progress toward your academic goals, but there is no time limit here!

Living life also equals learning, so engage him in farming, volunteering, swim class, or whatever doors are open, knowing that these are not lesser activities but part of the real work of education. As mentioned elsewhere, our own family found that some of our best test scores came after a year off of most formal schooling. Not what we would have planned, but a very valuable insight.

Convergent & Divergent Thinking

What These Skills Are and Why They Matter

Have you considered the necessity of incorporating both convergent and divergent thinking into your learning time? Experts recognize these as the 2 major types of brain challenges every human encounters.

Does that just sound like a whole bunch of big words? No worries—let's break it down. Your child needs to be able to find the right answer when needed (math, medicine dosage) and also needs to be able to come up with a creative, unscripted answer when the situation warrants (art, architecture).

A child who can only find the "right" answer will be a rigid thinker who can't problem-solve well or think outside the box.

A child who only thinks creatively will not be able to follow procedures or do anything that involves math.

Photo: The Melendez Kids in Honduras

What Is Convergent Thinking?

Convergent thinking generally involves finding a single best answer and is important in the study of math and science. Convergent thinking is the backbone of the majority of curricula and is crucial for future engineers, doctors, and even parents. Much of daily life is a series of determining right and wrong answers, and standardized tests favor the convergent thinker. But when we pursue only convergent-rich curricula, we miss the equally vital arena of divergent thinking.

Is Divergent Thinking Different?

Yes! Divergent thinking encourages your child's mind to explore many possible solutions—maybe even ideas that aren't necessarily apparent at first. It is in use when he discovers that there is more than one way to build a bridge with blocks, to animate a movie, or even to complete a doodle. Radically different from read-and-regurgitate textbooks, not only are divergent activities intellectually stimulating, but kids love them too.

Make a Conscious Effort to Include Both in Your Curriculum

Admittedly, because most textbooks and even puzzles are designed for convergent thinking, you will need to make a conscious effort to expose your children to multiple opportunities for divergent thinking. This is imperative because both divergent and convergent thinking are necessary for critical thinking to be effective.

Why Doctors Need Both Skills

As an example, let's look at a medical doctor. A physician needs to be extraordinarily skilled at convergent thinking to dose medications correctly, diagnose life-threatening emergencies, and follow safety procedures to avoid infection.

However, the first person to wash his hands before surgery or to find a treatment for Ebola used divergent thinking. They were thinking outside of the usual box to solve the problem.

Some of the best doctors today are those who employ powerful convergent skills to accurately diagnose, paired with curiosity and divergent thinking to find the most effective or previously undiscovered treatment plans.

Convergent in Third Grade

From reading to math, the backbone of your curriculum this year is convergent. This makes sense because so much of learning at this level is marveling at facts. Sometimes there really is a right answer!

What Is Divergent in Third Grade?

If you think about it, these are the same skills a lawyer uses to find legal precedents for her case, a teacher uses to engage her classroom, or an airline pilot uses in the case of emergency. These tools all include strong divergent aspects to help your child become a well-rounded thinker:

- Möbi Math Game
- GraviTrax Deluxe Set
- Battle Sheep
- Have I Got a Story for You!
- Once A Pawn A Time

GraviTrax works both your child's convergent and divergent skills. As he recreates the exact models shown, he's working on convergent skills and so much more. But when he revises that model to solve a problem or builds his own designs, that's capitalizing on divergent learning.

Similarly, games like Möbi Max and Battle Sheep also include both elements. The fixed rules are the convergent portion, while the way in which you choose to play the game (which pieces you put where and at which point in the game) is uniquely divergent.

How Do I Fit This Much Reading into My Day?

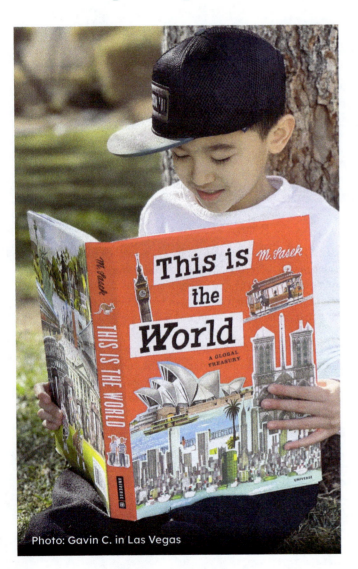

Photo: Gavin C. in Las Vegas

Here are 9 ideas to incorporate more reading into your family's busy schedule and unique schooling style:

1. Use Books of Various Lengths

A longer book than you'd usually pick may be perfect as an audiobook. On the flip side, if your child will be reading to a younger sibling or you are picking a new read-aloud for the whole gang, feel free to gear the book toward the younger participants, particularly if you're short on time.

2. Assign Independent Reading

This can be done in conjunction with quiet time or throughout the day. Our household often uses it as a strategy to calm the hyper and soothe the sad: I need you to go and snuggle into your favorite blanket and read one book and then come back ,and we'll try again. (Of course, your child does not need to be a competent reader yet to employ this strategy. Pictures may also be "read"!)

3. Quiet Time!

Does your family implement a quiet time already? Reading is a natural perk for that time. Quiet time can be as simple as setting a timer for 30 minutes (or more) and having your child relax with his favorite blanket or weighted lap pad and, of course, his book.

If it's possible for you to grab a book that you've been wanting to read and embrace the same plan, you'll be modeling what an ageless wonder reading can be. Of course, if your household is filled with little ones, it may be more practical for you to use this time for feeding babies or fixing dinner, and there's no shame in that, but consider your options as you plan your year.

4. Sneak Reading into Your Existing Routines

What routines are already going well for you? Could you incorporate a reading time into your existing bedtime routine, family devotions, car time, snack time, or other routine?

5. Audiobooks

Incorporate audiobooks and save the designated reader some time and energy. This is a particularly spectacular move for car time, art time, or puzzle time or even to smooth over particularly grumpy and hectic mealtimes.

6. Put the Busy Ones to Work

Encourage quiet activities such as puzzles, this year's STEM kit, or coloring while you read aloud or play the audiobook. It can be legitimately impossible for your kinesthetic learner to sit perfectly still and listen angelically, but break out the listening-time-only tools, and suddenly everyone looks forward to reading!

7. Brothers and Sisters

You don't have to be the only one reading to your child. Have your big kid read to a younger sibling as part of his school lessons. The older sibling will gain fluency as your younger one soaks up the one-on-one time. (No siblings in your home? How about cousins, playmates, grandparents, or even the family pet?)

8. Grandpa, Grandma, Aunties, Oh My!

Perhaps an auntie would welcome the opportunity to have Friday evenings be read-aloud time, complete with hot cocoa and scones. Or Grandma might love the idea of hosting all of her grandchildren once a month for a giant book party—each child could bring his favorite book to share. Too far away? Grandpa could record his favorite book (any audio recording app should work), then send the book to your child so that he can read along with Grandpa.

9. Get a Library Routine Going

Our family has loved reading since our toddler days, but we didn't use the library well until we settled into a simple routine. For us, that involves a central location for all library books and switching to a library branch with a slightly longer drive but more accessible hours. Those simple steps have quickly borne fruit with many more hours spent reading new books!

Help! My Book Says "Common Core"!

The Truth about Whether Your Timberdoodle Curriculum Kit Is Aligned with Common Core

Photo: The Glasman Family in Montana

There's been a lot of buzz, discussion, and anxiety in the homeschool community for more than a decade about the Common Core State Standards. Many of you have asked us what our stance is on the standards and whether our curriculum is designed to comply with them.

What Is the Common Core?

According to the CCSS website, "The Common Core State Standards Initiative is a state-led effort that established a single set of clear educational standards for kindergarten through 12th grade in English language arts and mathematics that states voluntarily adopt."

But Isn't That a Good Idea?

Growing up as an Air Force "brat," Deb, Timberdoodle's founder, attended many different schools throughout her educational career. She can tell you just how much easier it would have been for her if all of the schools had covered the same materials in the same order. Then she could have transferred effortlessly between them instead of missing critical information because the new school had already covered something her old school hadn't addressed yet. So yes, the concept may be brilliant, but there are some very valid concerns.

Why Homeschoolers Are Concerned

There is some real concern in the homeschooling community about what the Common Core Standards Initiative will mean to our families.

In an early article posted by the Homeschool Legal Defense Association, HSLDA Director of Federal Relations William Estrada wrote, "The CCSS specifically do not apply to private or homeschools….However, HSLDA has serious concerns with the rush to adopt the CCSS. HSLDA has fought national education standards for the past two decades. Why? National standards lead to national curriculum and national tests, and subsequent pressure on homeschool students to be taught from the same curricula."

Declining Quality?

Some in the homeschooling community have also expressed concern that as curriculum publishers endeavor to align with the CCSS, the educational quality in those texts will actually decrease rather than improve. Others are disenchanted with the atypical teaching methods employed by the CCSS, among other concerns.

What We Are Doing

At Timberdoodle, our approach is simple. We are ignoring the CCSS and continuing to search out crazy-smart curricula—exactly what we've been doing since 1985. Our specialty has always been hand-picking the best products in every subject area and offering the families who trust us the same products we have used or would happily use ourselves. And we have no plans to change the way we carefully review every resource we sell.

Some Products Do Say "Common Core"

Some of the items in almost every kit do, in fact, align with the CCSS. Not because we've sought that out but because the quality resources we've chosen for our curriculum are already up to that standard or beyond. It is no surprise to us that the excellent tools we are excited about are also good enough to exceed the qualifications for the CCSS.

This Has Never Changed and Will Not Change Now

At Timberdoodle, we work with trusted publishers and products we review carefully—not just in math and language arts but in all subject areas—so that we feel confident we are providing some of the best resources available for your children. Every time an item we've loved is revised (or stamped "Common Core"), we make sure that it has not been watered down or made confusing. Our goal is to exceed educational requirements, not by aligning our curriculum with any government standard but by continuing to find products that work well and meet the high standards we hold for our families and yours.

I Need a Homeschool Group, Right?

Community vs. Co-ops and More

No doubt you're familiar with some homeschool curricula that demand that their families form a group, take turns teaching, and meet weekly to press forward together. You may even wonder why you don't see pop-up Timberdoodle groups across the country/world.

This is a great question! The answer is very simple. You don't need one. Timberdoodle kits stand alone and are not teacher-intensive, meaning you can do it yourself and likely will!

Setting Your Own Pace—The Good

If you customized your kit at all, or if you have adjusted your schedule to your own life, it will make sense to you that your child does not need to be bound to any other child's progress. This is a huge goal of homeschooling: untether your child to proceed at precisely his own pace.

Setting Your Own Pace—The Bad

However, completely isolating yourself from other homeschoolers is far from ideal as well. You may not realize that the attention-span issues you are experiencing are completely age-appropriate or that it is atypical for your first-grader to be unable to follow a story without a lot of help.

Perhaps more importantly, there is a bit of good peer pressure for you in the form of community. If you are a relaxed "we'll do that next week" kind of person, it may be extremely helpful to have a friend asking you if you ever did get around to it and how it went.

Setting Your Own Pace—The Ugly

We are designed for community, and without it, the ugly side shows. From families who seem to care only about themselves to children who don't know how to interact with others, isolation is challenging on many fronts. COVID has certainly highlighted that for all of us!

We need each other, and we need to be deeply in each other's lives in order to flourish.

So Should I Start a Homeschool Group?

You could. And it could be lovely! But first take a look at your goals. Here are some that might apply:

- spend time with people I respect
- invest in others (Kids in your community? Parents who could use a mentor?)
- engage my kids with people who are different from them
- learn some skills
- have friends in real life, not just on social media
- team up for the parts of homeschooling I find stressful
- be encouraged to read widely
- get outside more

So many more ideas could be added! What things do you hope for this year, outside of finishing the materials in your kit? Once you know your goals, pick a format that works well for you and get the ball rolling.

Community Starters

- Start a group that meets at a different local park every Tuesday at noon. Pack lunch and enjoy some time with local moms and kids. Make a group text or other low-key way to make sure everyone knows they are welcome and knows which weeks are where.
- Join a local Facebook group that hosts several kid-friendly hikes a month. Participate those you can.
- Capitalize on P.E. and set aside time and money for ballet class, karate, or swim lessons this year.
- Find your local therapeutic riding / hippotherapy program and see if your horse-crazy teens could volunteer as sidewalkers.
- Google your child's interests. Is there a cooking class you could take together? Perhaps a theater club is starting, or a robotics camp?
- Don't despair if you, like us, find yourself limited by the ages or special needs of your children. A Zoom book study scheduled for after the children are in bed might be just the community you need.
- Buddy up! Look for opportunities for your children to serve. Can they help first-graders practice reading? Assist in after-school programming down the street? Take art or cookies to the local nursing home or shut-in every week? Assist a widow with yard work on Friday afternoons? Your opportunities will vary widely based on your children's ages and abilities, along with local needs. But this is well worth thinking through!
- If you've been involved with the foster care system, you know how critical and yet how draining it can be. Can you team up with a local family to bring lunch once a week and hang out with the kids for a few hours? Or could your teens go help teach younger children a skill? We had a teen come over each week to teach our little girls ballet. Not only is her relationship a huge investment in the girls' lives, but the fact that she comes here is a tremendous blessing as we juggle our erratic schedules and more medically complex little ones.
- Or, if you are that foster family, could you invite a local lonely grandmother-type to join you right in the crazy mess every Monday afternoon for art or reading time?
- Feel like you really need some accountability this year? Ask a friend if she'd be willing to go through your weekly checklists with you each Saturday morning and help you grow in your teaching skills / consistency.
- Make Thursday your Friends & Soup Night and have a standing invitation for friends to join you when possible.

Principles to Keep in Mind

If you're going to set a goal (e.g., get outside more with others), make a specific plan for doing that. (We will take a walk every morning at 9:00, and we will invite families A, B, and C to join us and invite their friends whenever they can.)

You aren't looking for perfection. You won't be able to meet every single week or complete every project you start. Don't panic if you're missing your walk this week because the baby has a doctor appointment or if you woke up with a cold and need to cancel swimming today. But if you make that your exception rather than your norm, you will see tremendous growth this year!

We all need community, but what it "should" look like in each family is something for you to decide, not us. Choose your adventure and get started. We suspect you'll find it is an amazing part of your routine!

Item-Specific Resources

Mosdos Opal Weekly Assignments

A Sample Detailed Schedule

Here's one way to break down your assignments to flow easily through a 30-week schedule. The page numbers refer to the current student reader as of this printing.

You'll notice that some weeks have more titles assigned than others. We've taken into account the number of corresponding workbook pages and the length of the readings to come up with these weekly assignments, but you should always feel free to rearrange in whatever fashion works for you. The surrounding content (e.g., introductory matter or sidebars) varies too, and your mathematically inclined student will quickly notice that no 2 weeks have identical page counts. Remind him that this is a good time to learn how to be flexible and persistent. After all, he may even find that the longer stories end up being his favorites!

Please note that you need to complete only as many of the corresponding activity pages and assignments as you determine to be appropriate for your reader. Our family would have chosen to answer the Studying the Selection questions in the readers orally rather than in writing. We would also likely skip the writing assignments since you'll be covering writing systematically with *Daily 6–Trait Writing*.

Book 1: Sunflower

Unit 1: All about the Story!

Week 1
Lesson in Literature...What Is a Story? - page 2
The Jar of Tassai - page 4
The Secret - page 16
Activity pages and assignments

Week 2
Lesson in Literature...What Is Plot? - page 18
The Story of the White Sombrero - page 20
Activity pages and assignments

Week 3
Lesson in Literature...What Are Characters? - page 36
A Cane in Her Hand - page 38
I Go Forth to Move about the Earth - page 48
Activity pages and assignments

Week 4
Lesson in Literature...What Is Setting? - page 50
Boom Town - page 52
General Store - page 66
Jill's Journal: On Assignment in Rhyolite, Nevada
            - page 68
Activity pages and assignments

Unit 2: All about the Plot!

Unit 3: All about the Characters!

Book 2: Daisy

Unit 4: All about Setting!

Unit 5: All about Theme!

Unit 6: The Grand Finalé

Now celebrate! You've made your way through a very rich year's study of literature!

Photo: The Whitaker Family in Unalaska, Alaska

The Reading Challenge

Reading Challenge Questions & Answers

Practical Details to Set Up a Productive Routine

So you love the idea of the reading challenge, but you'd like a boost to get you started? You've come to the right place!

Customize This!

You'll find a few ideas here for each challenge, but don't forget that you're not bound to our list. There are literally hundreds more options that may be even better for your family. Use these pages as starter ideas, not as your final list.

Will I See the Same Books Over and Over?

No! Each grade has its own reading challenge, so it will be rare to see the same book appear in multiple places, even across grades.

You might see some books repeated, but not too often. Each grade has its own set of books to read, so most books won't show up in multiple places, though about 25% might appear in more than one grade. This happens if a book fits really well in different challenges.

However, many books within your grade could fit into more than one category, but we only list them in one place within your challenges to make it easier for you. So if you want to read more than one book from a certain challenge, you'll probably find another challenge that fits the book if you skim through the list.

Photo: The Coulter Family in New Jersey

A Variety of Reading Levels

As you probably guessed, these are a mix of books to read to your child and books that he will read himself. Read-alouds meet your child's tremendous need for literacy, language, and stories, giving him a strong sense of why he wants to learn to read.

Notes about Our Book Ideas

If you've been reading to your child long (or if you've perused your local public library), you've probably noticed that families have very different standards for their reading materials. The books we've listed here are ones that members of our team have read, have added to their "I want to read this" list, or have had recommended to them.

Even among our team there is a wide range in what titles our families would find acceptable. Some of us find fantasy objectionable but will gladly read a scarier adventure story than other families would be comfortable with. Others of us consider those fantasy titles to be an interesting addition and worthy of much discussion!

Similarly, some of us prefer to avoid titles with troublesome language, bad attitudes, or other concerns, while others prefer to read and discuss them. We've opted to include titles with abandon, knowing that you can flip through them at the library to determine if they are a good fit for your family.

This is not a "Timberdoodle would sell these books if we could" list. We can't vouch for each of the titles, and we certainly can't know which ones are a good fit for your particular family. We even include titles with things we don't like, knowing that what is a "burn the book" moment for one family is a discussion starter for others. And if ever there was a time for deep discussion around many topics, this is that time!

We also are not above editing on the fly. If a book will be helpful for our kids except for a particular line, we'll often edit that line out as we read aloud. This would likely be a poor solution for permanent bookshelf residents, but it's perfect for library books!

Mostly we're providing this list to give you some ideas, just in case you're drawing a blank in thinking of books for a particular topic. Use these ideas as the jumping-off point for which they are intended, and, as always, we highly recommend previewing the books yourself.

Use Your Library

We can't overemphasize how useful your local library will be to you this year. Now that most libraries allow you to place books on hold online, you'll find that you can use any spare hour in your day to request books for the next challenges,

and then whoever is in town next can swing by the library and pick them up. If you've not yet become a dedicated library user, start now!

When we checked, roughly half of these books were available in some format from our local library. Since each library's selection varies, we've opted to keep them all listed here knowing that your selection will be different from ours.

If you have Kindle Unlimited or Everand, you will have still another library to choose from.

Reading and Talking

If you're newer to reading together, our biggest tips for you are these. First, just read together. Whether you read through one book a month or several a day, you are making memories and enjoying stories together.

Second, make sure you're discussing what you're reading. This doesn't need to be a formal book report on every book you encounter (please no!) or a tedious question-and-answer session every evening. Instead, talk as you go about the character qualities you see displayed, the kindnesses done (and undone), and the problems being solved. What does your child like about the book? What would he change if he could? If he was a character, which one would he be?

Simple questions build connection, emotional intelligence, worldview, logic, observational skills, and so much more.

Photo: The Panakkal Family in Texas

Reading and Racism

It is worth noting that many of the books we grew up on have terrible racist undertones (e.g., the neighbor in *Little House on the Prairie* who announces that "the only good Indian is a dead Indian" or those Tintin titles which portray people of color in negative ways). We have kept some of these titles on our reading list because racism is a crucial issue to discuss thoughtfully with your child, rather than just pretending it doesn't exist.

What Can You Do: Teaching Your Family To Be Anti-Racist by Tasha

Being anti-racist requires intentional and continuous action on your part as a mom. You set the tone for your home. Your children see what you truly value and believe. Waiting for "the right time" or when your child is "old enough" will be too late.

1. Point out racism in movies and literature. Classics especially. Think Little House on the Prairie *for a minute. Dr. Seuss.* To Kill a Mockingbird. Adventures of Huckleberry Finn. *I am not saying don't have these books on your shelves, but I am saying read them with your child and discuss why the author depicted the People of Color in those negative or rude ways.*

2. Discuss hard stuff. You should always be explicit with children, of all ages, that racism is very hurtful and always wrong. Teach your child to be an ally. Teach them to speak up when they hear someone saying racist comments or jokes. Teach them to be a friend to the refugees, the low-income kids, the disabled kids, the Hispanic kids, etc., etc.

3. Diversify your shelves. Find books and movies about People of Color, preferably where the storyline isn't about diversity. Continuously expose your child to the beauty and richness of the world—the peoples, cultures, religions, buildings, fashions, and foods. Watch the hard things. Read hard books. Don't shy away from the hard conversations.

4. Don't make racist jokes. Period. Racist jokes are so hurtful because they are basically saying, "You are so far beneath me, I can both conceal and express my prejudice and you can't do anything about it because it's socially acceptable—it's 'only' a joke."

We've quoted Tasha (previously a Timberdoodle blogger) here with her permission. Thank you, Tasha!

Reading and Gender Bias

Have you ever reflected that girls are commonly expected to enjoy books with both male and female protagonists, while boys are told that books featuring girls are "girl books" and unworthy of their attention? (Want to read up on this? See the thought-provoking book *A Place to Belong* by Amber O'Neal Johnston.)

I'm not talking about following interests here. By all means your dragon lover should enjoy books on dragons and your artsy person will appreciate books detailing technique. (And in our household it is a girl who loves the dragon books and a boy who is a particularly gifted artist.)

So what do I mean? Don't relegate books with female heroes to the girls' shelves. Just as girls enjoy books with male heroes, boys can and should enjoy books featuring female heroines. Enjoy each book for its content and teach your boys that yes, girls (and their stories) matter and are worthy of their time and attention.

Make This List Even Better

We love your book recommendations and feedback! Did you find a book you loved this year? We'd love to add your recommendations! Just shoot us a note at books@timberdoodle.com and let us know. Or were you perhaps disenchanted with one of our suggestions? Please let us know!

At the end of the year, fill out the Book Awards page near the end of this handbook and submit that. We'll be thrilled to credit you 50 Doodle Dollar reward points (worth $2.50 off your next order) as our thank-you for taking the time to share.

Tracking Your Reading Challenge

Can You Completely Fill This In?

If you're doing the topics out of order, check off completed topics as you go, and you'll be able to tell at a glance which topics are left. Across the page, color in 1 book after completing each week's reading to see your progress through the challenge at a glance. You can also record your book choices using the chart on each topic's page. If you prefer a printable version of the progress tracker, please visit your Timberdoodle.com account for your printable download. You can even print it poster-sized! (Didn't order directly from Timberdoodle.com? Contact us with your order number, and we'll get you set up!)

Reading Challenge Topics

Topic	
Mysteries/Detectives	☐
Reading	☐
Canada	☐
Jobs	☐
School	☐
Architecture	☐
World Leaders	☐
American Folktales	☐
Music	☐
Adventure	☐
Pilgrims	☐
Disasters	☐
Victorian England	☐
Economics	☐
Christmas	☐
Inventions	☐
Camping/Hiking	☐
Antarctica	☐

Topic	
Ballgames	☐
American Colonies	☐
American Founders	☐
American Revolution	☐
American Government	☐
Medicine	☐
War of 1812	☐
Australia	☐
American Symbols / Landmarks	☐
American Trailblazers	☐
Pirates	☐
South America	☐
Slavery / Underground Railroad	☐
Pioneers/Settlers	☐
Native Americans	☐
Texas/Mexico	☐
Railroads/Trains	☐
Gold Rush	☐

Mysteries/Detectives

Challenge 1

A to Z Mysteries series by Ron Roy

The Adventures of Sherlock Holmes retold from the Sir Arthur Conan Doyle original (Classic Starts)

Aven Green: Sleuthing Machine by Dusti Bowling

Ballpark Mysteries series by David A. Kelly

Bobbsey Twins series by Laura Lee Hope

Boxcar Children series by Gertrude Chandler Warner

Brixton Brothers series by Mac Barnett

Cam Jansen series by David A. Adler

Casebusters series by Joan Lowery Nixon

The Case of the Elevator Duck by Polly Berrien (Stepping Stones)

Detective Gordon series by Ulf Nilsson

Dino Detective and Awesome Possum, Private Eyes series by Tadgh Bentley

Encyclopedia Brown series by Donald J. Sobol

Fabio: The World's Greatest Flamingo Detective series by Laura James

Freddy the Detective by Walter R. Brooks

The Great Mouse Detective series by Eve Titus

The Happy Hollisters series by Jerry West

Hardy Boys Clue Books series by Franklin W. Dixon

The Hardy Boys Secret Files series by Franklin W. Dixon

InvestiGators series by John Patrick Green

Ivy and Bean Take the Case by Annie Barrows

Judy Moody, Girl Detective by Megan McDonald

King and Kayla series by Dori Hillestad Butler

Mac B., Kid Spy series by Mac Barnett

Mercy Watson Fights Crime by Kate DiCamillo

Mysteries according to Humphrey by Betty G. Birney

Mysteries of Sherlock Holmes by Sir Arthur Conan Doyle, adapted by Judith Conaway (Stepping Stones)

Nancy Clancy, Super Sleuth by Jane O'Connor

Nancy Drew and the Clue Crew series by Carolyn Keene

Nate the Great series by Marjorie Weinman Sharmat

Pedro's Mystery Club by Fran Manushkin

The Polk Street Mysteries by Patricia Reilly Giff

Pup Detectives series by Felix Gumpaw

Rider Woofson series by Walker Styles

Third-Grade Detectives series by George E. Stanley

Trixie Belden series by Julie Campbell or Kathryn Kenny

Whodunit Detective Agency series by Martin Widmark

	The Book You Chose	**Date Completed**
1.1 *Light Reader*		
1.2 *Interested Reader*		
1.3 *Avid Reader*		
1.4 *Committed Reader*		
1.5 *Enthralled Reader*		

Reading

Challenge 2

The Absent Author by Ron Roy (A to Z Mysteries)

Amelia Bedelia, Bookworm by Herman Parish

Beyond Little Women: A Story about Louisa May Alcott by Susan Bivin Aller (Creative Minds)

The Book Itch: Freedom, Truth, and Harlem's Greatest Bookstore by Vaunda Micheaux Nelson

Clara and the Bookwagon by Nancy Smiler Levinson (I Can Read)

The Country Artist: A Story about Beatrix Potter by David R. Collins (Creative Minds)

The Crook Who Took the Book by Carolyn Keene (Nancy Drew Notebooks)

Definitely Dominguita series by Terry Catasus Jennings

The Deserted Library Mystery by Gertrude Chandler Warner (The Boxcar Children)

Everybody Is Somebody by Henry Winkler (Here's Hank)

The Ghostwriter Secret by Mac Barnett (Brixton Brothers)

Judy Moody, Book Quiz Whiz by Megan McDonald

Laura Ingalls Wilder: Young Pioneer by Beatrice Gormley (Childhood of Famous Americans)

Library Mouse by Daniel Kirk

Louisa May Alcott: Young Novelist by Beatrice Gormley (Childhood of Famous Americans)

Lumber Camp Library by Natalie Kinsey-Warnock

Mark Twain: Young Writer by Miriam E. Mason (Childhood of Famous Americans)

More Than Anything Else by Marie Bradby

The Mystery Bookstore by Gertrude Chandler Warner (The Boxcar Children)

Once Upon a Thriller by Carolyn Keene (Nancy Drew Diaries)

Palace of Books by Patricia Polacco

Pickle Puss by Patricia Reilly Giff (Kids of the Polk Street School)

Planting Stories: The Life of Librarian and Storyteller Pura Belpré by Anika Aldamuy Denise

The Reading Race by Abby Klein (Ready, Freddy!)

Schomburg: The Man Who Built a Library by Carole Boston Weatherford

Thomas Jefferson Builds a Library by Barb Rosenstock

Undercover Bookworms by Franklin W. Dixon (Hardy Boys Clue Book)

Waiting for the Biblioburro by Monica Brown

Wh at Is the Story of Alice in Wonderland? by DanaMeachen Rau (Who HQ)

What Is the Story of Anne of Green Gables? by Ellen Labrecque (Who HQ)

What Is the Story of Nancy Drew? by Dana Meachen Rau (Who HQ)

What Is the Story of Willy Wonka? by Steve Korte (Who HQ)

What Is the Story of The Wizard of Oz? by Kirsten Anderson (Who HQ)

Who Was Laura Ingalls Wilder? by Patricia Brennan Demuth (Who HQ)

Who Was Mark Twain? by April Jones Prince (Who HQ)

Who Was Roald Dahl? by True Kelley (Who HQ)

The Year of the Book by Andrea Cheng (Anna Wang)

You Wouldn't Want to Live without Books! by Alex Woolf

	The Book You Chose	Date Completed
2.1 *Light Reader*		
2.2 *Interested Reader*		
2.3 *Avid Reader*		
2.4 *Committed Reader*		
2.5 *Enthralled Reader*		

Canada

Challenge 3

Anne of Green Gables by L.M. Montgomery, adapted by Deborah Felder (Stepping Stones)

Anne of Green Gables retold from the L.M. Montgomery original (Classic Starts)

Canada by William Anthony (Welcome to My World)

Canada by Jessica Dean (All Around the World)

Canada by Adam Markovics (Countries We Come From)

Canada by Julie Murray (Explore the Countries)

Canada by Nathan Olson (A Question and Answer Book)

Canada by Elma Schemenauer (Countries: Faces and Places)

Canada by Colleen Sexton (Exploring Countries)

Catching Spring by Sylvia Olsen (Orca Young Readers)

Champlain by Christopher Moore

The Creature in Ogopogo Lake by Gertrude Chandler Warner (The Boxcar Children)

Crossing Niagara: The Death-Defying Tightrope Adventures of the Great Blondin by Matt Tavares (Candlewick Biographies)

Cultural Traditions in Canada by Molly Aloian

Discovering Emily by Jacqueline Pearce (Orca Young Readers)

Ellie's New Home by Becky Citra (Orca Young Readers)

Emily's Dream by Jacqueline Pearce (Orca Young Readers)

Field Trip to Niagara Falls by Geronimo Stilton

Follow Me around Canada by Wiley Blevins

Growing Up in Wild Horse Canyon by Karen Autio

The Happy Hollisters and the Ice Carnival Mystery by Jerry West

The Happy Hollisters and the Mystery of the Midnight Trolls by Jerry West

The Happy Hollisters at Snowflake Camp by Jerry West

Hidden Mountain by Franklin W. Dixon (Hardy Boys)

The Intrepid Canadian Expedition by Jeff Brown (Flat Stanley's Worldwide Adventures)

The Island Horse by Susan Hughes

The Kids Book of Aboriginal Peoples in Canada by Diane Silvey

The Kids Book of Canada by Barbara Greenwood

The Kids Book of Canadian History by Carlotta Hacker

The Last Loon by Rebecca Upjohn (Orca Young Readers)

Let's Look at Canada by Joy Frisch-Schmoll

Let's Visit Vancouver! by Lisa Manzione (The Adventures of Bella and Harry)

Loonies and Toonies: A Canadian Number Book by Michael Ulmer

Lucky's Mountain by Dianne Maycock (Orca Young Readers)

M Is for Maple: A Canadian Alphabet by Michael Ulmer

M Is for Mountie: A Royal Canadian Mounted Police Alphabet by Polly Horvath

Milligan Creek series by Kevin Miller

Murphy and Mousetrap by Sylvia Olsen (Orca Young Readers)

The Mystery of the Calgary Stampede by Gertrude Chandler Warner (The Boxcar Children)

The Mystery of the Northern Lights by Carol Marsh (Around the World in 80 Mysteries)

Next Stop: Canada by Ginger McDonnell (Time for Kids)

The Niagara Falls Mystery by Gertrude Chandler Warner (The Boxcar Children)

No Way Out by Franklin W. Dixon (Hardy Boys)

Not My Girl by Christy Jordan-Fenton and Margaret Pokiak-Fenton

Owls in the Family by Farley Mowat

Paddle-to-the-Sea by Holling Clancy Holling

Poachers in the Pingos by Anita Daher (Orca Young Readers)
Polar Bear Puzzle by Amanda Lumry (Adventures of Riley)
Samuel de Champlain by Elizabeth MacLeod (Kids Can Read)
Samuel de Champlain: Father of the New France (Dissected Lives)
Star in the Storm by Joan Hiatt Harlow
Strawberry Moon by Becky Citra (Orca Young Readers)
The Sugaring–Off Party by Jonathan London

Summer in the City by Marie-Louise Gay and David Homel
Survival in the Wilderness by Steven Otfinoski
Thea Stilton and the Niagara Splash by Thea Stilton
Under a Prairie Sky by Anne Laurel Carter
The Viking Symbol Mystery by Franklin W. Dixon (Hardy Boys)
The Voyageur's Paddle by Kathy-job Wargin
Weird but True! Canada: 300 Outrageous Facts about the True North by Chelsea Lin (National Geographic Kids)
Yossi's Goal by Ellen Schwartz (Orca Young Readers)

	The Book You Chose	Date Completed
3.1 Light Reader		
3.2 Interested Reader		
3.3 Avid Reader		
3.4 Committed Reader		
3.5 Enthralled Reader		

Jobs or Careers

Challenge 4

100 Things to Be When You Grow Up by Lisa Gerry (National Geographic Kids)

Alone in His Teacher's House by Louis Sachar (Marvin Redpost)

Amelia Bedelia Cleans Up by Herman Parish

Amelia Bedelia On the Job by Herman Parish

Animal Control Officer by Lisa Harkrader (Jobs with Animals)

Animator by Jessica Cohn (Cutting Edge Cool Careers)

Astronomers by Ruth Owen (Out of the Lab: Extreme Jobs in Science)

Babysitting Bandit by Carolyn Keene (Nancy Drew and the Clue Crew)

Benny Uncovers a Mystery by Gertrude Chandler Warner (The Boxcar Children)

Cave Geologists by Christine Honders (Out of the Lab: Extreme Jobs in Science)

Climatologists and Meteorologists by Ruth Owen (Out of the Lab: Extreme Jobs in Science)

Emergency Rescue: Meet Real-Life Heroes! by Camilla Gersh (DK Readers)

Fashion Buyer by Jessica Cohn (Cutting Edge Cool Careers)

Fighter Pilots by Clara Cella (Dangerous Jobs)

Good Job, Kanani by Lisa Yee (American Girl)

Growing an Artist: The Story of a Landscaper and His Son by John Parra

Horse Riding Instructor by Lisa Harkrader (Jobs with Animals)

I Like Animals...What Jobs Are There? by Steve Martin (That's a Job?)

I Like Art...What Jobs Are There? by Susie Hodge (That's a Job?)

I Like Helping People...What Jobs Are There? by Amanda Learmonth (That's a Job?)

I Like Sports...What Jobs Are There? by Steve Martin (That's a Job?)

I Like the Outdoors...What Jobs Are There? by Carron Brown (That's a Job?)

I Want to Be in Sales When I Grow Up! by John Barrows

Ice Road Truckers by Clara Cella (Dangerous Jobs)

If I Were a Park Ranger by Catherine Stier

If I Were President by Catherine Stier

Ivy and Bean Get to Work! by Annie Barrows

J.D. and the Family Business by J. Dillard

J.D. and the Great Barber Battle by J. Dillard

A Job for Jenny Archer by Ellen Conford

Jobs by Joanna Brundle (A Look at Life Around the World)

Katie Finds a Job by Fran Manushkin (Katie Woo)

Lanie by Jane Kurtz (American Girl)

The Lemonade Raid by Carolyn Keene (Nancy Drew Notebooks)

The Marigold Mess by Jacqueline Jules (Sofia Martinez)

Marine Biologists by Ruth Owen (Out of the Lab: Extreme Jobs in Science)

Marion Takes Charge by Callie Barkley (The Critter Club)

Mindy Kim and the Yummy Seaweed Business by Lyla Lee

My Job in Engineering by Joanna Brundle (Classroom to Career)

My Job in Math by Joanna Brundle (Classroom to Career)

My Job in Science by Joanna Brundle (Classroom to Career)

My Job in Technology by Joanna Brundle (Classroom to Career)

My Vida Loca by Jacqueline Jules (Sofia Martinez)

Nerdy Jobs in STEM: 21 Careers in Science, Technology, Engineering, and Math that Make it Cool to Be Smart by Noreen Raines

On the Job at a Farm by Jessica Cohn

On the Job at School by Jessica Cohn

On the Job in a Restaurant by Jessica Cohn

On the Job in Construction by Jessica Cohn

On the Job in the Game by Jessica Cohn

On the Job in the Theatre by Jessica Cohn

Paleontologists and Archaelogists by Ruth Owen (Out of the Lab: Extreme Jobs in Science)

Park Naturalist by Lisa Harkrader (Jobs with Animals)

Pest Control Worker by Jessica Cohn (Dirty and Dangerous Jobs)

Race Car Drivers by Clara Cella (Dangerous Jobs)

Smoke Jumpers by Clara Cella (Dangerous Jobs)

Stunt Performers by Clara Cella (Dangerous Jobs)

Underwater Construction Workers by Clara Cella (Dangerous Jobs)

Up and Down the River by Rebecca Caudill (Fairchild Family)

Volcanologists and Seismologists by Ruth Owen (Out of the Lab: Extreme Jobs in Science)

What Do You Do If You Work at the Zoo? by Steve Jenkins and Robin Page

When I Grow Up by Al Yankovic

Who Will I Be? by Abby Huntsman

Wild Work! Animal Trainers by Jessica Cohn (Time for Kids)

World's Coolest Jobs by Anna Brett (Lonely Planet Kids)

Zoologists and Ecologists by Ruth Owen (Out of the Lab: Extreme Jobs in Science)

	The Book You Chose	Date Completed
4.1 *Light Reader*		
4.2 *Interested Reader*		
4.3 *Avid Reader*		
4.4 *Committed Reader*		
4.5 *Enthralled Reader*		

School

Challenge 5

Addy Learns a Lesson by Connie Porter (American Girl)

B Is for Betsy by Carolyn Haywood

Back to School with Betsy by Carolyn Haywood

Benjamin Pratt and the Keepers of the School series by Andrew Clements

The Best Worst School Year Ever by Barbara Robinson

Booker T. Washington by Thomas Amper (On My Own Biography)

The Carver Chronicles series by Karen English

Class Act by Kelly Starling Lyons (Jada Jones)

Ellray Jakes series by Sally Warner

A Fabumouse School Adventure by Geronimo Stilton

Felicity Learns a Lesson by Valerie Tripp (American Girl)

The Gatdget War by Betsy Duffey

The First Day of School Mystery by David A. Adler (Cam Jansen)

Freedom's School by Lesa Cline-Ransome

Gooney Bird Greene series by Lois Lowry

Hey, New Kid! by Betsy Duffey

Hidden in the Haunted School by Gertrude Chandler Warner (The Boxcar Children)

Horrible Harry Moves Up to Third Grade by Suzy Kline

How Not to Start Third Grade by Cathy Hapka (Step Into Reading)

How to Be Cool in the Third Grade by Betsy Duffey

A Hunger for Learning: A Story about Booker T. Washington by Gwenyth Swain (Creative Minds)

Ippie Unschooled by Nicole Olson

Jake Drake, Bully Buster by Andrew Clements

Jake Drake, Class Clown by Andrew Clements

Jake Drake, Know-It-All by Andrew Clements

Jake Drake, Teacher's Pet by Andrew Clements

Josefina Learns a Lesson by Valerie Tripp (American Girl)

Katie Woo Loves School by Fran Manushkin

Kirsten Learns a Lesson by Janet Shaw (American Girl)

Kit Learns a Lesson by Valerie Tripp (American Girl)

The Littles Go to School by John Peterson

Mama, Why Am I Homeschooled? by Jacy Ruwe

Marvin and the Meanest Girl by Suzy Kline

The Math Wiz by Betsy Duffey

Miami Jackson Sees It Through by Patricia and Frederick McKissack (Stepping Stones)

Molly Learns a Lesson by Valerie Tripp (American Girl)

Mystery at School by Laura Lee Hope (The Bobbsey Twins)

Prairie School by Avi (I Can Read)

Prairie School by Lois Lenski (American Regional)

Ramona Quimby, Age 8 by Beverly Cleary

Ramona the Brave by Beverly Cleary

Ramona the Pest by Beverly Cleary

Ruby Bridges Goes to School: My True Story by Ruby Bridges

Samantha Learns a Lesson by Susan Adler (American Girl)

School Days by Erica Silverman (Cowgirl Kate and Cocoa)

School Days according to Humphrey by Betty G. Birney

Schools by Joanna Brundle (A Look at Life Around the World)

Schoolhouse in the Woods by Rebecca Caudill (Fairchild Family)

Schoolroom in the Parlor by Rebecca Caudill (Fairchild Family)

The Secret School by Avi

Shark School series by Davy Ocean

Stella Endicott and the Anything-Is-Possible Poem by Kate DiCamillo (Tales from Deckawoo Drive)

Thank You, Mr. Falker by Patricia Polacco

This Is My Home, This Is My School by Jonathan Bean

The Wheel on the School by Meindert DeJong

	The Book You Chose	Date Completed
5.1 *Light Reader*		
5.2 *Interested Reader*		
5.3 *Avid Reader*		
5.4 *Committed Reader*		
5.5 *Enthralled Reader*		

Architecture

Challenge 6

13 Architects Children Should Know by Florian Heine

13 Bridges Children Should Know by Brad Finger

13 Buildings Children Should Know by Annette Roeder

13 Skyscrapers Children Should Know by Brad Finger

100 Things to Know about Architecture by Louise O'Brien

Architect by Kate Moening (Blastoff Readers: Careers in STEM)

Atlas of Amazing Architecture by Peter Allen

Bridges by Katie Marsico (A True Book: Engineering)

Concrete: From the Ground Up by Larissa Theule

Fallingwater: The Building of Frank Lloyd Wright's Masterpiece by Marc Harshman

Farmhouse by Sophie Blackall

The Future Architect's Handbook by Barbara Beck

George Ferris' Grand Idea: The Ferris Wheel by Jenna Glatzer (The Story Behind the Name)

Great Streets of the World by Frauke Berchtig

The Great Wheel by Robert Lawson

Gustave Eiffel's Spectacular Idea: The Eiffel Tower by Sharon Katz Cooper (The Story Behind the Name)

The Happy Hollisters and the Mystery in Skyscraper City by Jerry West

How Do Bridges Not Fall Down? A Book about Architecture and Engineering by Jennifer Shand

How Emily Saved the Bridge by Frieda Wishinsky

How Was That Built? The Stories behind Awesome Structures by Roma Agrawal

Look at That Building! by Scot Ritchie (Exploring Our Community)

The Power of Architecture: 25 Modern Buildings from around the World by Annette Roeder

Roberto: The Insect Architect by Nina Laden

See Inside Bridges, Towers and Tunnels by Struan Reid (Usborne)

See Inside Famous Buildings by Rob Lloyd Jones and Barry Ablett (Usborne)

See Inside Houses Long Ago by Rob Lloyd Jones and Barry Ablett (Usborne)

Shah Jahan by Souren Roy

Sky High by Patricia Reilly Giff

Skyscrapers by Libby Romero (National Geographic Kids)

Tree House Mystery by Gertrude Chandler Warner (The Boxcar Children)

Where Is the Brooklyn Bridge? by Megan Stine (Who HQ)

Where Is the Eiffel Tower? by Dina Anastasio (Who HQ)

Where Is the Empire State Building? by Janet B. Pascal (Who HQ)

Where Is the Taj Mahal? by Dorothy Hoobler (Who HQ)

Who Was Frank Lloyd Wright? by Ellen Labrecque (Who HQ)

Wild Buildings and Bridges: Architecture Inspired by Nature by Etta Kaner

You Wouldn't Want to Be a Skyscraper Builder! by John Malam

You Wouldn't Want to Work on the Brooklyn Bridge! by Tom Ratliff

	The Book You Chose	**Date Completed**
6.1 *Light Reader*		
6.2 *Interested Reader*		
6.3 *Avid Reader*		
6.4 *Committed Reader*		
6.5 *Enthralled Reader*		

Early Modern World Leaders

Challenge 7

The Actor, the Rebel and the Wrinkled Queen by Terry Deary (Tudor Tales)

Don't Know Much about Kings and Queens of England by Kenneth C. Davis

Elizabeth and the Royal Pony by Joan Holub (Young Princesses Around the World)

Elizabeth I by Richard Brassey (Brilliant Brits)

Elizabeth I by Nel Yomtov (A True Book)

Elizabeth I and the Spanish Armada by Colin Hynson (Stories from History)

Elizabeth I: The Outcast Who Became England's Queen by Simon Adams (National Geographic Kids)

Elizabeth I, the People's Queen: Her Life and Times by Kerrie Logan Hollihan

George vs George: The American Revolution as Seen from Both Sides by Rosalyn Schanzer

Good Queen Bess: The Story of Elizabeth I of England by Diane Stanley

I Am Queen Nzinga: The Great Queen Warrior by Amina Phelps

If You Were Me and Lived in Elizabethan England by Carole P. Roman

The Kidnapped Prince: The Life of Olaudah Equiano by Olaudah Equiano, adapted by Ann Cameron

King Louie's Shoes by D.J. Steinberg

The King's Day: Louis XIV of France by Aliki

The Maid, the Witch and the Cruel Queen by Terry Deary (Tudor Tales)

Mary, Queen of Scots by Fiona Macdonald (Kids in History)

Mary, Queen of Scots: Escape from Lochleven Castle by Theresa Breslin

Napoleon by Lucy Lethbridge (Usborne)

Nelson by Richard Brassey (Brilliant Brits)

Nelson by Minna Lacey (Usborne)

Njinga of Ndongo and Matamba by Ekiuwa Aire (Our Ancestries)

Nzingha: The Great Warrior of Angola by Desree Crooks

Peter the Great by Diane Stanley

A Picture Book of Simón Bolívar by David A. Adler

A Picture Story of Napoleon by J. de Marthold

The Pirate Queen by Terry Deary (Pirate Tales)

A Royal Ride: Catherine the Great's Great Invention by Kristen Fulton

Shah Jahan by Souren Roy

Tudors and Stuarts (Ladybird Histories)

The Tudors: Kings, Queens, Scribes, and Ferrets! by Marcia Williams

Who Was Catherine the Great? by Pam Pollack and Meg Belviso (Who HQ)

Who Was Napoleon? by Jim Gigliotti (Who HQ)

Who Was Queen Elizabeth? by June Eding (Who HQ)

You Wouldn't Want to Be Mary Queen of Scots! by Fiona Macdonald

	The Book You Chose	Date Completed
7.1 *Light Reader*		
7.2 *Interested Reader*		
7.3 *Avid Reader*		
7.4 *Committed Reader*		
7.5 *Enthralled Reader*		

American Folklore

Challenge 8

The Adventures of Brer Rabbit and Friends from Stories Collected by Joel Chandler Harris retold by Karima Amin (DK)

American Tall Tales by Mary Pope Osborne

American Tall Tales by Adrien Stoutenburg

Calamity Jane by Stephen Krensky (On My Own)

Calamity Jane retold by Larry Dane Brimner

The Classic Tales of Brer Rabbit by Joel Chandler Harris

The Favorite Uncle Remus by Joel Chandler Harris and A. B. Frost

John Henry by Jane H. Gould (Jr. Graphic American Legends)

John Henry: Hammerin' Hero by Stephanie True Peters (Graphic Spin)

John Henry by Julius Lester

John Henry by Stephen Krensky (On My Own Folklore)

The Legend of the Lady's Slipper by Kathy-jo Wargin

Mike Fink by Stephen Krensky (On My Own)

Mike Fink: A Tall Tale retold and illustrated by Steven Kellogg

More Tales of Uncle Remus: Further Adventures of Brer Rabbit, His Friends, Enemies, and Others as told by Julius Lester

Native American Animal Stories told by Joseph Bruchac

North American Indian Tales by W. T. Larned (Dover Children's Thrift Classics)

Paul Bunyan by Steven Kellogg

Paul Bunyan by Andrea P. Smith (Jr. Graphic American Legends)

Paul Bunyan: A Tall Tale retold and illustrated by Stephen Krensky (On My Own)

Paul Bunyan and Other Tall Tales by Jane B. Mason (Scholastic Junior Classics)

Paul Bunyan's Sweetheart by Marybeth Lorbiecki

Pecos Bill by Bill Balcziak

Pecos Bill by David L. Ferrell (Jr. Graphic American Legends)

Pecos Bill by Stephen Krensky (On My Own)

Pecos Bill: A Tall Tale retold and illustrated by Steven Kellogg

Pecos Bill: Colossal Cowboy by Sean Tulien (Graphic Spin)

Pecos Bill: The Greatest Cowboy of All Time by James Cloyd Bowman

The People Could Fly: American Black Folktales told by Virginia Hamilton

A Picture Book of Davy Crockett by David A. Adler

Porch Lies: Tales of Slicksters, Tricksters, and Other Wily Characters by Patricia McKissack

Sally Ann Thunder Ann Whirlwind Crockett: A Tall Tale retold and illustrated by Steven Kellogg

The Tales of Uncle Remus: The Adventures of Brer Rabbit as told by Julius Lester

The Tall Tale of Paul Bunyan by Martin Powell (Graphic Spin)

Thunder Rose by Jerdine Nolen

	The Book You Chose	**Date Completed**
8.1 Light Reader		
8.2 Interested Reader		
8.3 Avid Reader		
8.4 Committed Reader		
8.5 Enthralled Reader		

Music

Challenge 9

Anna Maria's Gift by Janice Shefelman (Stepping Stones)

Aven Green: Music Machine by Dusti Bowling

Becoming Bach by Tom Leonard

Before There Was Mozart: The Story of Joseph Boulogne, Chevalier de Saint–George by Lesa Cline-Ransome

Bold Composer: A Story about Ludwig van Beethoven by Judith P. Josephson (Creative Minds)

Eugenia Lincoln and the Unexpected Package by Kate DiCamillo (Tales from Deckawoo Drive)

Franz Schubert and His Merry Friends by Opal Wheeler and Sybil Deucher (Zeezok Great Musicians)

Frederic Chopin, Son of Poland by Opal Wheeler (Zeezok Great Musicians)

Getting to Know the World's Greatest Composers series by Mike Venezia

Her Piano Sang: A Story about Clara Schumann by Barbara Allman (Creative Minds)

Hey, Charleston! The True Story of the Jenkins Orphanage Band by Anne Rockwell

A Horn for Louis by Eric A. Kimmel (Stepping Stones)

Irving Berlin: The Immigrant Boy Who Made America Sing by Nancy Churnin

Karen's Tuba by Ann M. Martin (Baby-Sitters Little Sister)

Katie's Noisy Music by Fran Manushkin (Katie Woo)

Ludwig Beethoven and the Chiming Tower Bells by Opal Wheeler (Zeezok Great Musicians)

Mahalia Jackson: Young Gospel Singer by Montrew Dunham (Childhood of Famous Americans)

Making the Band by Martha Maker (Craftily Ever After)

Mice Take the Stage by Thea Stilton (Mouseford Academy)

Moonlight on the Magic Flute by Mary Pope Osborne (Magic Tree House)

Mozart: The Boy Who Changed the World With His Music by Marcus Weeks (National Geographic Kids)

Mozart the Wonder Boy by Opal Wheeler (Zeezok Great Musicians)

Music and How It Works: The Complete Guide for Kids by Charlie Morland (DK)

Musical Genius: A Story about Wolfgang Amadeus Mozart by Barbara Allen (Creative Minds)

A Musical Mess by Carolyn Keene (Nancy Drew and the Clue Crew)

The Mystery of the Stolen Music by Gertrude Chandler Warner (The Boxcar Children)

Never Stop Singing by Denise Lewis Patrick (American Girl: Melody)

No Ordinary Sound by Denise Lewis Patrick (American Girl: Melody)

Peter Tchaikovsky and the Nutcracker Ballet by Opal Wheeler (Zeezok Great Musicians)

Play It Again, Mozart! by Geronimo Stilton

Play, Louis, Play! The True Story of a Boy and His Horn by Muriel Harris Weinstein

Raggin': A Story about Scott Joplin by Barbara Mitchell (Creative Minds)

A Rockin' Mystery by Franklin W. Dixon (The Hardy Boys Secret Files)

The Rock 'n' Roll Mystery by Gertrude Chandler Warner (The Boxcar Children)

Sarai Saves the Music by Sarai Gonzalez and Monica Brown

Sebastian Bach, the Boy from Thuringia by Opal Wheeler and Sybil Deucher (Zeezok Great Musicians)

Singing Sensation by Geronimo Stilton

The Singing Suspects by Carolyn Keene (Nancy Drew Notebooks)

Sing to the Stars by Mary Brigid Barrett

V Is for von Trapp: A Musical Family Alphabet by William Anderson

Who Was Duke Ellington? by M.D. Payne (Who HQ)

Who Was Louis Armstrong? by Yona Zeldis McDonough (Who HQ)

Who Was Wolfgang Amadeus Mozart? by Yona Zeldis McDonough (Who HQ)

Wolfgang Amadus Mozart by Barbara Catchpole (Kids in History)

Write On, Irving Berlin! by Leslie Kimmelman

	The Book You Chose	Date Completed
9.1 *Light Reader*		
9.2 *Interested Reader*		
9.3 *Avid Reader*		
9.4 *Committed Reader*		
9.5 *Enthralled Reader*		

Adventure

Challenge 10

100 Cupboards by N. D. Wilson

Adventure according to Humphrey by Betty G. Birney

The Adventures of Huckleberry Finn retold from the Mark Twain original by Oliver Ho (Classic Starts)

The Adventures of Pippi Longstocking by Astrid Lindgren

The Adventures of Tom Sawyer by Mark Twain, adapted by Monica Kulling (Stepping Stones)

The Adventures of Tom Sawyer retold from the Mark Twain original (Classic Starts)

Andy and Sandy's Anything Adventure by Tomie dePaola

Bear Grylls Adventures series

Big Foot and Little Foot by Ellen Potter

The Castle in the Attic by Elizabeth Winthrop

Cece Loves Science and Adventure by Kimberly Derting

Extreme Ice Adventure by Jake Maddox

Flat Stanley's Worldwide Adventures series by Jeff Brown

Geronimo Stilton series

Ginger Pye by Eleanor Estes

Half Magic by Edward Eager

The Happy Hollisters at Lizard Cove by Jerry West

Huckleberry Dog by Alexander Steele (The Adventures of Wishbone)

Lottie Lipton Adventures series by Dan Metcalf

Navigation by Jenny Mason (A True Book: Survival Skills)

Nick and Tesla's High-Voltage Danger Lab series by Bob Plugfelder and Steve Hocksmith

Obstacle Challenge by Jake Maddox

Ragweed by Avi

River Race by Jake Maddox

Robinson Crusoe retold from the Daniel Defoe original (Classic Starts)

Surprise Island by Gertrude Chandler Warner (The Boxcar Children)

Swiss Family Robinson by Johann Wyss, adapted by Daisy Alberto

The Swiss Family Robinson retold from the Johann David Wyss original (Classic Starts)

The Swiss Family Robinson (graphic novel edition)

The Tale of Despereaux by Kate DeCamillo

Terror in the Caverns by Jake Maddox

Totally True Adventures! series by various authors

The Wingfeather Saga series by Andrew Peterson

The Wonderful Flight to the Mushroom Planet by Eleanor Cameron

	The Book You Chose	**Date Completed**
10.1 *Light Reader*		
10.2 *Interested Reader*		
10.3 *Avid Reader*		
10.4 *Committed Reader*		
10.5 *Enthralled Reader*		

Pilgrims

Challenge 11

Across the Wide Dark Sea: The Mayflower Journey by Jean Van Leeuwen

Constance and the Dangerous Crossing: A Mayflower Survival Story by Julie Gilbert (Girls Survive)

Dash by Kate Klimo (Dog Diaries)

Don't Know Much about the Pilgrims by Kenneth C. Davis

The First Thanksgiving by Jean Craighead George

If You Lived During the Plimoth Thanksgiving by Chris Newell

If You Sailed on the Mayflower in 1620 by Ann McGovern

If You Were a Kid at the First Thanksgiving by Melissa Sarno

If You Were a Kid on the Mayflower by John Son

Life on the Mayflower by Jessica Gunderson

Mayflower 1620: A New Look at a Pilgrim Voyage by Plimoth Plantation with Peter Arenstam, John Kemp, and Catherine O'Neill Grace (National Geographic)

Mayflower Treasure Hunt by Ron Roy (A to Z Mysteries)

My Life in the Plymouth Colony by Max Caswell (My Place in History)

The Mystery at Plymouth Rock by Carole Marsh (Real Kids, Real Places)

Pilgrim Cat by Carol Antoinette Peacock

Pilgrim Stories by Margaret Pumphrey

Pilgrims by Mary Pope Osborne (Magic Tree House Fact Tracker)

The Pilgrims at Plymouth by Lucille Recht Penner

The Pilgrims' First Thanksgiving by Jessica Gunderson

The Pilgrims of Plimoth by Marcia Sewall

Pilgrims of Plymouth by Susan E. Goodman (National Geographic)

The Pilgrims' Voyage to America by Thomas Kingsley Troupe (A Fly on the Wall History)

Sailing on the Mayflower by Jessica Rusick (This or That? History Edition)

Samuel Eaton's Day: A Day in the Life of a Pilgrim Boy by Kate Waters

Sarah Morton's Day: A Day in the Life of a Pilgrim Girl by Kate Waters

Squanto: A Friend to the Pilgrims by Carol Ghiglieri (Easy Reader Biographies)

Squanto and the First Thanksgiving by Joyce C. Kessel (On My Own)

Squanto's Journey: The Story of the First Thanksgiving by Joseph Bruchac

Tapenum's Day: A Wampanoag Indian Boy in Pilgrim Times by Kate Waters

Thanksgiving on Plymouth Plantation by Diane Stanley (Time-Traveling Twins)

Thanksgiving on Thursday by Mary Pope Osborne (Magic Tree House)

The Thanksgiving Story by Alice Dalgliesh

Three Young Pilgrims by Cheryl Harness

The Voyage of the Mayflower by Allison Lassieur (Graphic Library)

What Was the First Thanksgiving? by Joan Holub (Who HQ)

Who's That Stepping on Plymouth Rock? by Jean Fritz

You Wouldn't Want to Sail on the Mayflower! by Peter Cook

	The Book You Chose	Date Completed
11.1 *Light Reader*		
11.2 *Interested Reader*		
11.3 *Avid Reader*		
11.4 *Committed Reader*		
11.5 *Enthralled Reader*		

Disasters in History

Challenge 12

Aboard the Titanic by John H. Son (A True Book: The Titanic)

Alice on the Island: A Pearl Harbor Survival Story by Mayumi Shimose Poe (Girls Survive)

All Stations! Distress! April 15, 1912: The Day the Titanic Sank by Don Brown (Actual Times)

Apollo 13: How Three Brave Astronauts Survived a Space Disaster by Kathleen Weidner Zoehfeld (Totally True Adventures)

The Apollo 13 Mission by Kassandra Radomski (Fact Finders)

Attack on Pearl Harbor by Kate Messner (Ranger in Time)

Audrey under the Big Top: A Hartford Circus Fire Survival Story by Jessica Gunderson (Girls Survive)

Carrie and the Great Storm: A Galveston Hurricane Survival Story by Jessica Gunderson (Girls Survive)

Cinders by Kate Klimo (Horse Diaries)

Disaster on the Titanic by Kate Messner (Ranger in Time)

Disasters in History 8-book compilation

Donner Dinner Party by Nathan Hale (Hazardous Tales)

The Earthshaking Earthquake Mystery by Carole Marsh (Masters of Disasters)

Emmi in the City: A Great Chicago Fire Survival Story by Salima Alikhan (Girls Survive)

The Endurance: Shackleton's Perilous Expedition in Antarctica by Meredith Hooper

Escape from the Great Earthquake by Kate Messner (Ranger in Time)

Escape from the Twin Towers by Kate Messner (Ranger in Time)

The Ferocious Forest Fire Mystery by Carole Marsh (Masters of Disasters)

Fire at the Triangle Factory by Holly Littlefield (On My Own)

Fire in the Sky: A Tale of the Hindenburg Explosion by J. Gunderson

Hindenburg by Jenny Fretland Van Voorst (Pogo: Man-Made Disasters)

The History of Pearl Harbor by Susan B. Katz (A World War II Book for New Readers)

The History of the Titanic by Kelly Milner Halls

Hurricane Katrina, 2005 by John Albert Torres (Natural Disasters)

Hurricane Katrina Rescue by Kate Messner (Ranger in Time)

I Escaped the California Camp Fire by Scott Peters

I Escaped the Donner Party by Scott Peters

I Survived Hurricane Katrina, 2005 by Lauren Tarshis

I Survived the Attacks of September 11, 2001 by Lauren Tarshis

I Survived the Bombing of Pearl Harbor, 1941 by Lauren Tarshis

I Survived the California Wildfires, 2018 by Lauren Tarshis

I Survived the Destruction of Pompeii, AD 79 by Lauren Tarshis

I Survived the Eruption of Mount St. Helens, 1980 by Lauren Tarshis

I Survived the Galveston Hurricane, 1900 by Lauren Tarshis

I Survived the Great Chicago Fire, 1871 by Lauren Tarshis

I Survived the Great Molasses Flood, 1919 by Lauren Tarshis

I Survived the Hindenberg Disaster, 1937 by Lauren Tarshis

I Survived the Japanese Tsunami, 2011 by Lauren Tarshis

I Survived the Joplin Tornado, 2011 by Lauren Tarshis

I Survived the San Francisco Earthquake, 1906 by Lauren Tarshis

I Survived the Sinking of the Titanic, 1912 by Lauren Tarshis

Ice Wreck by Lucille Recht Penner (Stepping Stones)

The Johnstown Flood, 1889 by Dan Leathers (Natural Disasters)

Leah Braves the Flood: A Great Molasses Flood Survival Story by Julie Kathleen Gilbert (Girls Survive)

Lily and the Great Quake: A San Francisco Earthquake Survival Story by Veeda Bybee (Girls Survive)

Lost in Outer Space: The Incredible Journey of Apollo 13 by Tod Olson

Lost in the Antarctic: The Doomed Voyage of the Endurance by Tod Olson

Lost in the Pacific, 1942: Not a Drop to Drink by Tod Olson

Lucy Fights the Flames: A Triangle Shirtwaist Factory Survival Story by Julie Gilbert (Girls Survive)

Maribel Versus the Volcano: A Mount St. Helens Survival Story by Sarah Hannah Gomez (Girls Survive)

Noelle at Sea: A Titanic Survival Story by Nikki Shannon Smith (Girls Survive)

Pearl Harbor by Stephen Krensky (Ready-to-Read)

Pearl Harbor by Nancy Ohlin (Blast Back!)

The Rescue Adventure of Stenny Green, Hindenburg Crash Eyewitness by Candice Ransom (History's Kid Heroes)

The Rooftop Adventure of Minnie and Tessa, Factory Fire Survivors by Holly Littlefield (History's Kid Heroes)

The Shackleton Sabotage by Gertrude Chandler Warner (The Boxcar Children)

The Sinking of the Titanic by Matt Doeden (Graphic Library)

Sparky by Kate Klimo (Dog Diaries)

Stay Alive: The Journal of Douglas Allen Deeds, Donner Party Expedition, 1846 by Rodman Philbrick (My Name Is America)

Sunny by Kate Klimo (Dog Diaries)

Tara and the Towering Wave: An Indian Ocean Tsunami Survival Story by Cristina Oxtra (Girls Survive)

Tornado Outbreak, 1985 by Dan Leathers (Natural Disasters)

The Voracious Volcano Mystery by Carole Marsh (Masters of Disasters)

What Was Hurricane Katrina? by Robin Koontz (Who HQ)

What Was Pearl Harbor? by Patricia Brennan Demuth (Who HQ)

What Was Pompeii? by Jim O'Connor (Who HQ)

What Was the Great Chicago Fire? by Janet B. Pascal (Who HQ)

What Was the Hindenburg? by Janet B. Pascal (Who HQ)

What Was the San Francisco Earthquake? by Dorothy Hoobler (Who HQ)

What Was the Titanic? by Stephanie Sabol (Who HQ)

What Were the Twin Towers? by Jim O'Connor (Who HQ)

You Wouldn't Want to Be on Apollo 13! by Ian Graham

You Wouldn't Want to Be on Shackleton's Polar Expedition! by Jen Green

You Wouldn't Want to Be on the Hindenburg! by Ian Graham

	The Book You Chose	**Date Completed**
12.1 Light Reader		
12.2 Interested Reader		
12.3 Avid Reader		
12.4 Committed Reader		
12.5 Enthralled Reader		

Victorian England

Challenge 13

Alexander Graham Bell: Master of Sound by Ann Hood (The Treasure Chest)

Burn: Michael Faraday's Candle by Darcy Pattison (Moments in Science)

The Cheshire Cheese Cat: A Dickens of a Tale by Carmen Agra Deedy

Charles Dickens and Friends: Five Lively Retellings by Marcia Williams

The Fabulous Flyer by Terry Deary (Victorian Tales)

George Mueller: Faith to Feed Ten Thousand by Renee Taft Meloche (Heroes for Young Readers)

Great Expectations by Charles Dickens, adapted by Monica Kulling (Stepping Stones)

Great Expectations retold from the Charles Dickens original (Classic Starts)

Little Lord Fauntleroy retold from the Frances Hodgson Burnett orginal (Classic Starts)

A Little Princess by Frances Hodgson Burnett, adapted by Cathy East Dubowski (Stepping Stones)

A Little Princess retold from the Frances Hodgson Burnett original (Classic Starts)

Oliver Twist by Joanne Mattern (Wishbone Classics)

Oliver Twist retold from the Charles Dickens original (Classic Starts)

Queen Victoria's Bathing Machine by Gloria Whelan

Rags and Riches by Mary Pope Osborne (Magic Tree House Fact Tracker)

The Sea Monsters by Terry Deary (Victorian Tales)

The Secret Garden by Frances Hodgson Burnett, adapted by James Howe (Stepping Stones)

The Secret Garden retold from the Frances Hodgson Burnett original (Classic Starts)

Tales for Hard Times: A Story about Charles Dickens by David R. Collins (Creative Minds)

Thursday's Child by Noel Streatfeild

Tiny Tim by Kate Klimo (Dog Diaries)

The Twisted Tunnels by Terry Deary (Victorian Tales)

Victorian Britain by Jeremy Smith (100 Facts)

Victorians (Ladybird Histories)

What Is the Story of Ebenezer Scrooge? by Sheila Keenan (Who HQ)

Who Was Queen Victoria? by Jim Gigliotti (Who HQ)

You Wouldn't Want to Be a Victorian Miner! by John Malam

You Wouldn't Want to Be a Victorian Schoolchild! by John Malam

You Wouldn't Want to Be a Victorian Servant! by Fiona MacDonald

You Wouldn't Want to Work in a Victorian Mill! by John Malam

	The Book You Chose	**Date Completed**
13.1 Light Reader		
13.2 Interested Reader		
13.3 Avid Reader		
13.4 Committed Reader		
13.5 Enthralled Reader		

Economics

Challenge 14

Almost Zero by Nikki Grimes (Dyamonde Daniel)

Amelia Bedelia Means Business by Herman Parish

Breaking the Piggy Bank by Martha Maker (Craftily Ever After)

Count Your Money with the Polk Street School by Patricia Reilly Giff

The Everything Kids' Money Book: Earn It, Save It, and Watch It Grow! by Brette McWhorter Sember

Everything Money: A Wealth of Facts, Photos, and Fun! (National Geographic Kids)

Get to Know Money: A Fun, Visual Guide to How Money Works and How to Manage It by Kalpana Fitzpatrick (DK)

The Happy Hollisters and the Secret of the Lucky Coins by Jerry West

How Do Kids Make Money? A Book for Young Entrepreneurs by Kate Hayes

Lemonade for Sale by Stuart J. Murphy (MathStart)

Lunch Money by Andrew Clements

M Is for Money: An Economics Alphabet by Debbie and Michael Shoulders

Money by Joe Cribb (DK Eyewitness)

Money: What You Need to Know by Jill Sherman (Fact Files)

Money Basics series by Lisa Bullard

Mr. Chickee's Funny Money by Christopher Paul Curtis

Nancy Clancy Seeks a Fortune by Jane O'Connor

Not-So-Common Cent$: Super Duper Important Facts about Money You Can't Afford to Miss by Sarah Flynn

One Hen: How One Small Loan Made a Big Difference by Katie Smith Milway

The Penny Pot by Stuart J. Murphy (MathStart)

Piggy Bank Problems by Fran Manushkin (Katie Woo)

Prices! Prices! Prices! Why They Go Up and Down by David A. Adler

A Quick History of Money: From Bartering to Bitcoin by Clive Gifford

Sarai and the Meaning of Awesome by Sarai Gonzalez and Monica Brown

Shoeshine Girl by Clyde Robert Bulla

Show Me the Money: Big Questions about Finance by Alvin Hall (DK)

Spending Money by Jessica Cohn (A True Book: Money)

The Story of Money by Betsy Maestro

Thomas Sowell: A Self-Made Man by Sean B. Dickson (Heroes of Liberty)

Trouble at the Treasury by Ron Roy (Capital Mysteries)

What Can You Do with Money? Earning, Spending, and Saving by Jennifer S. Larson (Lightning Bolt)

What Banks Do With Money by Janet Liu and Melinda Liu (A True Book: Money)

What Can You Do With Money? Earning, Spending, and Saving by Jennifer S. Larson (Lightning Bolt)

What Do We Buy? A Look at Goods and Services by Robin Nelson (Lighting Bolt)

What Is Money? by Alicia Green (A True Book: Money)

Who Was Sam Walton? by James Buckley Jr. (Who HQ)

Who's Buying? Who's Selling? Understanding Consumers and Producers by Jennifer S. Larson (Lightning Bolt)

You Wouldn't Want to Live without Money! by Alex Woolf

The Book You Chose	**Date Completed**
14.1 *Light Reader*	
14.2 *Interested Reader*	
14.3 *Avid Reader*	
14.4 *Committed Reader*	
14.5 *Enthralled Reader*	

Christmas

Challenge 15

Addy's Surprise: A Christmas Story, 1864 by Connie Porter (American Girl)

Amelia Bedelia Wraps It Up by Herman Parish

Amy's Very Merry Christmas by Callie Barkley (The Critter Club)

Apple Tree Christmas by Trinka Hakes Noble

The Bells of Christmas by Virginia Hamilton

The Best ~~Worst~~ Christmas Pageant Ever by Barbara Robinson

Christmas around the World by Emily Kelley (On My Own Holidays)

A Christmas Carol by Charles Dickens

Christmas Day in the Morning by Pearl S. Buck

The Christmas Day Kitten by James Herriot

Christmas in Noisy Village by Astrid Lindgren

Christmas in the Country by Cynthia Rylant and Diane Goode

Christmas in the Trenches by John McCutcheon

A Christmas like Helen's by Natalie Kinsey-Warnock

The Christmas Miracle of Jonathan Toomey by Susan Wojciechowski

Christmas Tapestry by Patricia Polacco

The Christmas Tree Ship by Carol Crane

December Dog by Ron Roy (Calendar Mysteries)

December Secrets by Patricia Reilly Giff (Kids of the Polk Street School)

The Family under the Bridge by Natalie Savage Carlson

Felicity's Surprise: A Christmas Story, 1774 by Valerie Tripp (American Girl)

A Ghost Tale for Christmas Time by Mary Pope Osborne (Magic Tree House)

Gingerbread Jitters by Abby Klein (Ready, Freddy)

Goats for Christmas by Jacqueline Kelly (Calpurnia Tate: Girl Vet)

Horrible Harry and the Christmas Surprise by Suzy Kline

The House without a Christmas Tree by Gail Rock (Addie Mills)

I Saw Three Ships by Elizabeth Goudge

Jasmine's Christmas Ride by Bonnie Bryant (Pony Tails)

Jingle Bells by Catherine Hapka (Horse Diaries)

Josefina's Surprise: A Christmas Story, 1824 by Valerie Tripp (American Girl)

Kirsten's Surprise: A Christmas Story, 1854 by Janet Shaw (American Girl)

Kit's Surprise: A Christmas Story, 1934 by Valerie Tripp (American Girl)

The Last Holiday Concert by Andrew Clements

A Little House Christmas: Holiday Stories from the Little House Books by Laura Ingalls Wilder

Molly's Surprise: A Christmas Story, 1944 by Valerie Tripp (American Girl)

Mystery at the Christmas Market by Janelle Diller (Pack-n-Go Girls)

Nancy and Plum by Betty MacDonald

A Nancy Drew Christmas by Carolyn Keene (Nancy Drew Diaries)

Nate the Great and the Crunchy Christmas by Marjorie Weinman Sharmat

The Old-Fashioned Mystery by Carolyn Keene (Nancy Drew Notebooks)

Rosco the Rascal and the Holiday Lights by Shana Gorian

Samantha's Surprise: A Christmas Story, 1901 by Maxine Rose Schur (American Girl)

A Shiloh Christmas by Phyllis Reynolds Naylor

The True Gift by Patricia MacLachlan

The Twenty-Four Days before Christmas by Madeleine L'Engle (Austin Family Series)

The Vanderbeekers of 141st Street by Karina Yan Glaser

A Very Crazy Christmas by Abby Klein (Ready, Freddy)

A Very Merry Christmas by Geronimo Stilton

The White House Christmas Mystery by Carole Marsh (Real Kids, Real Places)

The Wounded Buzzard on Christmas Eve by John R. Erickson (Hank the Cowdog)

The Year of the Perfect Christmas Tree by Gloria Houston

	The Book You Chose	**Date Completed**
15.1 *Light Reader*		
15.2 *Interested Reader*		
15.3 *Avid Reader*		
15.4 *Committed Reader*		
15.5 *Enthralled Reader*		

Inventions

Challenge 16

Alexander Graham Bell by Barbara Kramer (National Geographic Kids)

Alexander Graham Bell by Stephanie Sammartino McPherson (History Maker Bios)

Alexander Graham Bell: A Famous Inventor by Justin McCory Martin (Easy Reader Biographies)

Alexander Graham Bell and the Telephone by Jennifer Fandel (Graphic Library)

Bell's Breakthrough by Stacia Deutsch and Rhody Cohon (Blast to the Past)

Ben Franklin and His First Kite by Stephen Krensky (Ready to Read: Childhood of Famous Americans)

Ben Franklin and the Magic Squares by Frank Murphy (Step Into Reading)

Ben Franklin Thinks Big by Sheila Keenan (I Can Read)

Ben Franklin's Big Splash: The Mostly True Story of His First Invention by Barb Rosenstock

Benjamin Franklin, American Genius: His Life and Ideas by Brandon Marie Miller

Benjamin Franklin: Inventor of the Nation! by Mark Shulman (Show Me History)

Brilliant Inventions by Mack Van Gageldonk (World of Wonder)

Click! A Story about George Eastman by Barbara Mitchell (Creative Minds)

Eli Whitney by Catherine A. Welch (History Maker Bios)

Flying Feet by Patricia Reilly Giff (Zigzag Kids)

Getting to Know the World's Greatest Inventors & Scientists series by Mike Venezia

George Eastman by Susan Bivin Aller (History Maker Bios)

George Eastman and the Kodak Camera by Jennifer Fandel (Graphic Library)

Great Black Heroes: Five Notable Inventors by Wade Hudson (Hello Reader)

A Head Full of Notions: A Story about Robert Fulton by Andy Russell Bowen (Creative Minds)

Henry Ford by Jeffrey Zuehlke (History Maker Bios)

Henry Ford and the Model T by Michael O'Hearn (Graphic Library)

How Ben Franklin Stole the Lightning by Rosalyn Schanzer

How Things Are Made by Oldrich Ruzicka

I Is for Idea: An Inventions Alphabet by Marcia Schonberg

Iqbal and His Ingenious Idea: How a Science Project Helps One Family and the Planet by Elizabeth Suneby (CitizenKid)

Inventions by Duncan Brewer (100 Facts)

Johann Gutenberg and the Printing Press by Kay Melchisedech Olson (Graphic Library)

Louis Pasteur and Pasteurization by Jennifer Fandel (Graphic Library)

Maker of Machines: A Story about Eli Whitney by Barbara Mitchell (Creative Minds)

Mesmerized: How Ben Franklin Solved a Mystery That Baffled All of France by Mara Rockliff

The Mystery at Kill Devil Hills by Carole Marsh (Real Kids, Real Places)

Now and Ben: The Modern Inventions of Benjamin Franklin by Gene Barretta

Philo Farnsworth and the Television by Ellen S. Niz (Graphic Library)

A Picture Book of Thomas Alva Edison by David A. Adler

Robert Fulton: Boy Craftsman by Marguerite Henry (Childhood of Famous Americans)

Samuel Morse and the Telegraph by David Seidman (Graphic Library)

The Secret Invention by Thea Stilton (Mouseford Academy)

See Inside Inventions by Alex Frith (Usborne)

Shoes for Everyone: A Story about Jan Matzeliger by Barbara Mitchell (Creative Minds)

Snaggle Doodles by Patricia Reilly Giff (Kids of the Polk Street School)

Steve Jobs, Steve Wozniak, and the Personal Computer by Donald B. Lemke (Graphic Library)

The Story of Henry Ford by Jenna Grodzicki (A Biography Book for New Readers)

The Story of the Wright Brothers by Annette Whipple (A Biography Book for New Readers)

Thomas Edison by Shannon Zemlicka (History Maker Bios)

Thomas Edison and the Lightbulb by Scott R. Welvaert (Graphic Library)

We'll Race You, Henry! A Story about Henry Ford by Barbara Mitchell (Creative Minds)

Who Was Alexander Graham Bell? by Bonnie Bader (Who HQ)

Who Was Henry Ford? by Michael Burgan (Who HQ)

Who Was Nikola Tesla? by Jim Gigliotti (Who HQ)

Who Was Thomas Alva Edison? by Margaret Frith (Who HQ)

Who Were the Wright Brothers? by James Buckley Jr. (Who HQ)

Whoosh! Lonnie Johnson's Super-Soaking Stream of Inventions by Chris Barton

Will and Orv by Walter A. Schulz (On My Own)

The Wright Brothers by Ginger Wadsworth (History Maker Bios)

The Wright Brothers and the Airplane by Xavier W. Niz (Graphic Library)

The Wright Brothers' First Flight by Thomas Kingsley Troupe (A Fly in the Wall History)

You Wouldn't Want to Be on the First Flying Machine! by Ian Graham

	The Book You Chose	**Date Completed**
16.1 Light Reader		
16.2 Interested Reader		
16.3 Avid Reader		
16.4 Committed Reader		
16.5 Enthralled Reader		

Camping/Hiking

Challenge 17

Alvin Ho: Allergic to Camping, Hiking, and Other Natural Disasters by Lenore Look

Backpacking Hacks: Camping Tips for Outdoor Adventures by Raymond Bean

Backyard Campout by Jerdine Nolen (Bradford Street Buddies)

Bears Beware by Patricia Reilly Giff (Zigzag Kids)

Cam Jansen and the Summer Camp Mysteries by David A. Adler

Camp Time in California by Mary Pope Osborne (Magic Tree House)

The Campground Kids series by C.R. Fulton

Camping Catastrophe! by Abby Klein (Ready, Freddy)

Camping Chaos by Franklin W. Dixon (The Hardy Boys Secret Files)

The Camping Trip by Catherine Hapka (Pony Scouts)

The Camp-Out Mystery by Gertrude Chandler Warner (The Boxcar Children)

Camp Time in California by Mary Pope Osborne (Magic Tree House)

The Canoe Trip Mystery by Gertrude Chandler Warner (The Boxcar Children)

The Case of the Cool-Itch Kid by Patricia Reilly Giff (Polk Street Mysteries)

The Case of the Lost Camp by John R. Erickson (Hank the Cowdog)

A Cheese-Colored Camper by Geronimo Stilton

The Day Camp Disaster by Carolyn Keene (Nancy Drew Notebooks)

Detective Camp by Ron Roy (A to Z Mysteries)

Emma Dilemma and the Camping Nanny by Patricia Hermes

Eva's Campfire Adventure by Rebecca Elliott (Owl Diaries)

Freddy Goes Camping by Walter R. Brooks

The Growling Bear Mystery by Gertrude Chandler Warner (The Boxcar Children)

The Happy Hollisters and the Scarecrow Mystery by Jerry West

Like Bug Juice on a Burger by Julie Sternberg

Liz at Marigold Lake by Callie Barkley (The Critter Club)

Mystery at Camp Survival by Gertrude Chandler Warner (The Boxcar Children)

Nature Lover by Kelly Starling Lyones (Jada Jones)

Rosco the Rascal Goes to Camp by Shana Gorian

Scavenger Hunt Heist by Franklin W. Dixon (Hardy Boys Clue Book)

Secret at Mystic Lake by Carolyn Keene (Nancy Drew Diaries)

Shadows of Caesar's Creek by Sharon M. Draper (Clubhouse Mysteries)

The Sign in the Smoke by Carolyn Keene (Nancy Drew Diaries)

The Soggy, Foggy Campout by Henry Winkler (Here's Hank)

Starry Skies and Fireflies by Jenny Meyerhoff (The Friendship Garden)

Survival for Beginners: A Step-by-Step Guide to Camping and Outdoor Skills by Colin Towell (DK)

Trail Trouble by Jake Maddox

Trouble at Camp Treehouse by Carolyn Keene (Nancy Drew Notebooks)

	The Book You Chose	Date Completed
17.1 *Light Reader*		
17.2 *Interested Reader*		
17.3 *Avid Reader*		
17.4 *Committed Reader*		
17.5 *Enthralled Reader*		

Antarctica

Challenge 18

Animals Robert Scott Saw: An Adventure in Antarctica by Sandra Markle

Ann and Liv Cross Antarctica by Ann Bancroft and Liv Arnesen

Antarctica by Lucy Bowman (Usborne Beginners)

Antarctica by Helen Cowcher

Antarctica by Madeline Donaldson (Pull Ahead Books: Continents)

Antarctica by Anita Ganeri (Introducing Continents)

Antarctica by Karen Kellaher (The Seven Continents)

Black Whiteness: Admiral Byrd Alone in the Antarctic by Robert Burleigh

Byrd and Igloo: A Polar Adventure by Samantha Seiple

Can You Survive Antarctica? An Interactive Survival Adventure by Rachael Teresa Hanel (You Choose)

Dreamy Antarctica by Maya Sara Karthik

Emperor Penguins by Deborah Lock (DK)

Emperor Penguins by Roberta Edwards (Penguin Young Readers)

Endurance in Antarctica by Katrina Charman (Survival Tails)

The Endurance: Shackleton's Perilous Expedition in Antarctica by Meredith Hooper

Escape from the Ice by Peter and Connie Roop (Hello, Reader)

Eve of the Emperor Penguin by Mary Pope Osborne (Magic Tree House)

First to the Last Place on Earth by Geronimo Stilton

Hooray for Antarctica! by April Pulley Sayre (Our Amazing Continents)

Ice Wreck by Lucille Recht Penner (Stepping Stones)

Introducing Antarctica by Anita Ganeri (Introducing Continents)

Life in a Frozen World: Wildlife of Antarctica by Mary Batten

Lost in the Antarctic: The Doomed Voyage of the Endurance by Tod Olson

Mr. Popper's Penguins by Richard and Florence Atwater

The Mystery in Icy Antarctica by Carole Marsh (Around the World in 80 Mysteries)

Penguin Puzzle by Judith Bauer Stamper (Magic School Bus Chapter Book)

Penguins and Antarctica by Mary Pope Osborne (Magic Tree House Fact Tracker)

Race to the South Pole by Kate Messner (Ranger in Time)

The Race to the South Pole by Jim Pipe (Stories from History)

Rescue in Antarctica by Emily Sohn (Graphic Library)

Sea of Ice: The Wreck of the Endurance by Monica Kulling (Step Into Reading)

The Search for Antarctic Dinosaurs by Sally M. Walker (On My Own)

Shackleton and the Lost Antarctic Expedition by Blake A. Hoena (Graphic Library)

The Shackleton Sabotage by Gertrude Chandler Warner (The Boxcar Children)

Shackleton's Journey by William Grill

Sophie Scott Goes South by Alison Lester

The South Pole by Nancy Dickmann (Explorer Tales)

Surviving Antarctica: Ernest Shackleton by Matt Doeden (They Survived)

Trapped by the Ice! Shackleton's Amazing Antarctica Adventure by Michael McCurdy

A Trip to the Bottom of the World with Mouse by Frank Viva (A Toon Book)

Waiting for Joey: An Antarctic Penguin Journal by Jean Pennycook

When the Sun Shines on Antarctica and Other Poems about the Frozen Continent by Irene Latham

Where Is Antarctica? by Sarah Fabiny (Who HQ)

Who Counts the Penguins? Working in Antarctica by Mary Meinking (Wild Work)

A Year in Antarctica by Anita Ganeri (DK iOpener)

You Wouldn't Want to Be on Shackleton's Polar Expedition! by Jen Green

	The Book You Chose	**Date Completed**
18.1 *Light Reader*		
18.2 *Interested Reader*		
18.3 *Avid Reader*		
18.4 *Committed Reader*		
18.5 *Enthralled Reader*		

Ballgames

Challenge 19

Baseball

The Babe and I by David A. Adler

Babe Ruth: Baseball's All-Time Best! by James Buckley Jr. (Show Me History)

Ball Park Mysteries series by David A. Kelly

Baseball by Mary Pope Osborne (Magic Tree House Fact Tracker)

The Baseball Adventure of Jackie Mitchell, Girl Pitcher vs. Babe Ruth by Jean L. S. Patrick (History's Kid Heroes)

The Baseball Mystery by Carole Marsh (Real Kids, Real Places)

Baseball's Best: Five True Stories by Andrew Gutelle (Step Into Reading)

Baseball's Greatest Hitters by S. A. Kramer (Step Into Reading)

Behind the Plate by Jake Maddox

A Big Day for Baseball by Mary Pope Osborne (Magic Tree House)

Ellie Steps Up to the Plate by Callie Barkley (The Critter Club)

The Home Run Mystery by Gertrude Chandler Warner (The Boxcar Children)

I Am on Strike against Softball by Julie Gassman (Sports Illustrated Kids)

Jackie Robinson by Stephanie Sammartino McPherson (History Maker Bios)

Jackie Robinson and the Story of All Black Baseball by Jim O'Connor (Step Into Reading)

Lou Gehrig: One of Baseball's Greatest by Guernsey Van Riper Jr. (Childhood of Famous Americans)

Lucky: Maris, Mantle, and My Best Summer Ever by Wes Tooke

The Magic School Bus Plays Ball by Joanna Cole

Miami Jackson Makes the Play by Patricia and Frederick McKissack (Stepping Stones)

The Missing Baseball by Mick Lupica (Zach and Zoe Mysteries)

The Missing Mitt by Franklin W. Dixon (The Hardy Boys Secret Files)

The Missing Playbook by Franklin W. Dixon (Hardy Boys Clue Book)

The Mystery at the Ballpark by Gertrude Chandler Warner (The Boxcar Children)

The Mystery of the Babe Ruth Baseball by David A. Adler (Cam Jansen)

Negro Leagues: All-Black Baseball by Laura Driscoll (Smart About History)

A Picture Book of Jackie Robinson by David A. Adler

Satchel Paige: Don't Look Back by David A. Adler

She Loved Baseball: The Effa Manley Story by Audrey Vernick

Something to Prove by Rob Skead

The Spy in the Bleachers by Gertrude Chandler Warner (The Boxcar Children)

Stolen Bases by Jake Maddox

The Story of Babe Ruth by Jenna Grodzicki (A Biography Book for Young Readers)

The Story of Jackie Robinson by Andrea Thorpe (A Biography Book for Young Readers)

The Streak: How Joe DiMaggio Became America's Hero by Barb Rosenstock

Strike-Out Scare by Carolyn Keene (Nancy Drew Notebooks)

There's No Crying in Baseball by Anita Yasuda (Sports Illustrated Kids)

The Unwilling Umpire by Ron Roy (A to Z Mysteries)

What Is the World Series? by Gail Herman (Who HQ)

What Were the Negro Leagues? by Varian Johnson (Who HQ)

Who Was Babe Ruth? by Joan Holub (Who HQ)

Who Was Jackie Robinson? by Gail Herman (Who HQ)

Who Was Roberto Clemente? by James Buckley Jr. (Who HQ)

Basketball

The Basketball Blowout by David A. Kelly (Most Valuable Players)

The Basketball Mystery by David A. Adler (Cam Jansen)

The Basketball Mystery by Gertrude Chandler Warner (The Boxcar Children)

Basketball's Greatest Players by S. A. Kramer (Step Into Reading)

Drive to the Hoop by Jake Maddox

EllRay Jakes Stands Tall by Sally Warner

Five Fouls and You're Out! by Val Priebe (Sports Illustrated Kids)

Full Court Dreams by Jake Maddox

Game Day: Jump Shot by David Sabino (Ready to Read)

The Half-Court Zero by Mike Lupica (Zach and Zoe Mysteries)

The Harlem Globetrotters Present the Points Behind Basketball by Larry Dobrow (Ready to Read: Science of Fun Stuff)

Here Come the Harlem Globetrotters by Larry Dobrow (Ready to Read)

Hoop Doctor by Jake Maddox

Little Shaq series by Shaquille O'Neal

Nobody Wants to Play with a Ball Hog by Julie Gassman (Sports Illustrated Kids)

Nothing But the Net by Jake Maddox

Over the Net by Jake Maddox

Rebound Time by Jake Maddox

The Superstar Story of the Harlem Globetrotters by Larry Dobrow (Ready to Read: History of Fun Stuff)

Football

Betsy and the Boys by Carolyn Haywood

The Dog That Stole Football Plays by Matt Christopher (Passport to Reading)

The Football Fiasco by Mike Lupica (Zach and Zoe Mysteries)

The Football Fumble by David A. Kelly (Most Valuable Players)

Football Triple Threat by Jake Maddox

Home-Field Football by Jake Maddox

A Running Back Can't Always Rush by Nate LeBoutillier (Sports Illustrated Kids)

Touchdown Triumph by Jake Maddox

What Is the Super Bowl? by Dina Anastasio (Who HQ)

	The Book You Chose	Date Completed
19.1 Light Reader		
19.2 Interested Reader		
19.3 Avid Reader		
19.4 Committed Reader		
19.5 Enthralled Reader		

American Colonies

Challenge 20

Building a New Land: African Americans in Colonial America by James Haskins

The Colonial Caper Mystery at Williamsburg by Carole Marsh (Real Kids, Real Places)

Crispus Attucks: Black Leader of Colonial Patriots by Dharathula H. Millender (Childhood of Famous Americans)

The Courage of Sarah Noble by Alice Dalgliesh

Digging Up the Past by Vivian Sathre (The Adventures of Wishbone)

The Double Life of Pocahontas by Jean Fritz

Fort Mose and the Story of the Man Who Built the First Free Black Settlement in Colonial America by Glennette Turner

Freedom Seeker: A Story about William Penn by Gwenyth Swain (Creative Minds)

I Escaped the Salem Witch Trials by Scott Peters

If You Lived in Colonial Times by Ann McGovern

If You Lived in Williamsburg in Colonial Days by Barbara Brenner

If You Were a Kid in the Thirteen Colonies by Wil Mara

If You Were Me and Lived in Colonial America by Carole P. Roman

James Towne: Struggle for Survival by Marcia Sewall

Kids in Colonial Times by Lisa A. Wroble (Kids Throughout History)

The Last of the Breed by Alexander Steele (The Adventures of Wishbone)

A Lion to Guard Us by Clyde Robert Bulla

Living in the Jamestown Colony by Jessica Rusick (This or That? History Edition)

The Lucky Sovereign by Stewart Lees

Molly Bannaky by Alice McGill

The Mystery at Jamestown by Carole Marsh (Real Kids, Real Places)

The Mystery of the Lost Colony by Carole Marsh (Real Kids, Real Places)

The Mystery of the Roanoke Colony by Xavier W. Niz (Graphic Library)

Our Strange New Land: Elizabeth's Jamestown Colony Diary by Patricia Hermes (My America)

Pocahontas by Ingri and Edgar Parin d'Aulaire

Pocahontas by Caryn Jenner (DK Readers)

Pocahontas: An American Princess by Joyce Milton (Penguin Young Readers)

Pocahontas and the Strangers by Clyde Robert Bulla

Pocahontas: Young Peacemaker by Leslie Gourse (Childhood of Famous Americans)

Sailing to America: Colonists at Sea by James E. Knight (Adventures in Colonial America)

The Salem Witch Trials by Michael J. Martin (Graphic Library)

Sam Collier and the Founding of Jamestown by Candice Ransom (On My Own History)

Season of Promise: Elizabeth's Jamestown Colony Diary by Patricia Hermes (My America)

Seventh and Walnut: Life in Colonial Philadelphia by James E. Knight (Adventures in Colonial America)

The Starving Time: Elizabeth's Jamestown Colony Diary by Patricia Hermes (My America)

The Story of Jamestown by Eric Mark Braun (Graphic Library)

The Story of William Penn by Aliki

Traitor in Williamsburg: A Felicity Mystery by Elizabeth M. Jones (American Girl)

The True Story of Pocahontas by Lucille Recht Penner (Step Into Reading)

What Were the Salem Witch Trials? by Joan Holub (Who HQ)

William's House by Ginger Howard

You Wouldn't Want to Be an American Colonist! by Jacqueline Morley

Your Life as a Settler in Colonial America by Thomas Kingsley Troupe (The Way It Was)

	The Book You Chose	Date Completed
20.1 *Light Reader*		
20.2 *Interested Reader*		
20.3 *Avid Reader*		
20.4 *Committed Reader*		
20.5 *Enthralled Reader*		

American Founders

Challenge 21

Abigail Adams by Jane Sutcliffe (History Maker Bios)

Abigail Adams: First Lady of the American Revolution by Patricia Lakin (Ready to Read: Stories of Famous Americans)

Alexander Hamilton by James Buckley (DK Life Stories)

Alexander Hamilton by Libby Romero (National Geographic Kids)

Alexander Hamilton: American Hero by Barbara Lowell (Penguin Young Readers)

Alexander Hamilton: A Plan for America by Sarah Albee (I Can Read)

Alexander Hamilton: The Fighting Founding Father by Mark Shuman (Show Me History)

Alexander Hamilton: From Immigrant Boy to Founding Father by Joyce Claiborne-West (Heroes of Liberty)

Alexander Hamilton: From Orphan to Founding Father by Monica Kulling (Step Into Reading)

Alexander Hamilton: Little Lion by Ann Hood (The Treasure Chest)

Ben and Me: An Astonishing Life of Benjamin Franklin by His Good Mouse, Amos by Robert Lawson

Benjamin Franklin by Ingri and Edgar Parin d'Aulaire

Benjamin Franklin by Mary Pope Osborne (Magic Tree House Fact Tracker)

Don't Know Much about George Washington by Kenneth C. Davis

Don't Know Much about Thomas Jefferson by Kenneth C. Davis

Eliza Hamilton: Founding Mother by Monica Kulling (Step Into Reading)

Father of the Constitution: A Story about James Madison by Barbara Mitchell (Creative Minds)

George Washington: America's First President by Justin McCory Martin (Easy Reader Biographies)

George Washington by Caroline Crosson Gilpin (National Geographic Kids)

George Washington by Cheryl Harness (National Geographic)

George Washington by Ingri and Edgar Parin d'Aulaire

George Washington: An Illustrated Biography by David A. Adler

George Washington: First President by Mike Venezia (Getting to Know the U.S. Presidents)

George Washington: His Legacy of Faith, Character, and Courage by Demi

George Washington: Leading a New Nation by Matt Doeden (Graphic Library)

George Washington: Soldier and Statesman! by Mark Shulman (Show Me History)

George Washington: The First President by Sarah Albee (I Can Read)

I Am George Washington by Grace Norwich

John Adams by Jane Sutcliffe (History Maker Bios)

John Adams: Second President by Mike Venezia (Getting to Know the U.S. Presidents)

John Adams Speaks for Freedom by Deborah Hopkinson (Ready to Read: Stories of Famous Americans)

John Adams: Young Revolutionary by Jan Adkins (Childhood of Famous Americans)

Liberty or Death: A Story about Patrick Henry by Stephanie Sammartino McPherson (Creative Minds)

Meet George Washington by Joan Heilbroner (Landmark)

Meet Thomas Jefferson by Marvin Barrett (Landmark)

Nathan Hale: Patriot Spy by Shannon Zemlicka (On My Own)

Patrick Henry: Liberty or Death by Jason Glaser (Graphic Library)

Paul Revere by George Sullivan (In Their Own Words)

Paul Revere by Jane Sutcliffe (History Makers Bios)

Paul Revere: Boston Patriot by Augusta Stevenson (Childhood of Famous Americans)

A Picture Book of Alexander Hamilton by David A. Adler

A Picture Book of Benjamin Franklin by David A. Adler

A Picture Book of George Washington by David A. Adler

A Picture Book of John and Abigail Adams by David A. Adler

A Picture Book of John Hancock by David A. Adler

A Picture Book of Patrick Henry by David A. Adler

A Picture Book of Paul Revere by David A. Adler

A Picture Book of Samuel Adams by David A. Adler

A Picture Book of Thomas Jefferson by David A. Adler

The Remarkable Benjamin Franklin by Cheryl Harness (National Geographic)

Remember the Ladies: A Story about Abigail Adams by Jeri Ferris (Creative Minds)

The Revolutionary John Adams by Cheryl Harness (National Geographic)

The Story of Alexander Hamilton by Christine Platt (A Biography Book for New Readers)

The Story of Benjamin Franklin by Shannon Anderson (A Biography Book for New Readers)

The Story of Eliza Hamilton by Natasha Wing (A Biography Book for New Readers)

The Story of George Washington by Lisa Trusiani (A Biography Book for New Readers)

The Story of Thomas Jefferson by Lisa Trusiani (A Biography Book for New Readers)

Thomas Jefferson by Cheryl Harness (National Geographic)

Thomas Jefferson and the Ghostriders by Howard Goldsmith (Ready to Read: Childhood of Famous Americans)

Thomas Jefferson for Kids: His Life and Times by Brandon Marie Miller

Thomas Jefferson: Great American by Matt Doeden (Graphic Library)

Thomas Jefferson: Life, Liberty, and the Pursuit of Everything by Maira Kalman

Thomas Jefferson: Third President by Mike Venezia (Getting to Know the U.S. Presidents)

Thomas Paine and the Dangerous Word by Sarah Jane Marsh

Uncommon Revolutionary: A Story about Thomas Paine by Laura Hamilton Waxman (Creative Minds)

Who Was Alexander Hamilton? by Pam Pollack (Who HQ)

Who Was Ben Franklin? by Dennis Brindell Fradin (Who HQ)

Who Was George Washington? by Roberta Edwards (Who HQ)

Who Was Paul Revere? by Roberta Edwards (Who HQ)

Who Was Thomas Jefferson? by Dennis Brindell Fradin (Who HQ)

	The Book You Chose	Date Completed
21.1 Light Reader		
21.2 Interested Reader		
21.3 Avid Reader		
21.4 Committed Reader		
21.5 Enthralled Reader		

American Revolution

Challenge 2

The 18 Penny Goose by Sally M. Walker

American Revolution by Mary Pope Osborne (Magic Tree House Fact Tracker)

The American Revolution by Nancy Ohlin (Blast Back)

And Then What Happened, Paul Revere? by Jean Fritz

Answering the Cry for Freedom: Stories of African Americans and the American Revolution by Gretchen Woelfle

The Black Regiment of the American Revolution by Linda Crotta Brennan

The Boston Massacre by Michael Burgan (Graphic Library)

The Boston Tea Party by Matt Doeden (Graphic Library)

The Boston Tea Party by Rebecca Paley (American Girl)

Buttons for General Washington by Peter and Connie Roop (On My Own)

Felicity series by Valerie Tripp (American Girl)

Five Smooth Stones: Hope's Revolutionary War Diary by Kristiana Gregory (My America)

The Founding Fathers Were Spies! by Patricia Lakin (Ready to Read: Secrets of American History)

A Free Woman on God's Earth: The True Story of Elizabeth "Mumbet" Freeman, the Slave Who Won Her Freedom by Jana Laiz and Ann-Elizabeth Barnes

George Washington and the General's Dog by Frank Murphy (Step Into Reading)

George Washington's Breakfast by Jean Fritz

George Washington's Spies by Claudia Friddell (Totally True Adventures)

Hannah of Fairfield by Jean Van Leeuwen

Heroes of the Revolution by David A. Adler

The History of the American Revolution by Emma Carlson Berne (A History Book for New Readers)

The Horse-Riding Adventure of Sybil Ludington, Revolutionary War Messenger by Marsha Amstel (History's Kid Heroes)

I Have Not Yet Begun to Fight: A Story about John Paul Jones by Elaine Marie Alphin (Creative Minds)

I Survived the American Revolution by Lauren Tarshis

If You Grew Up with George Washington by Ruth Belov Gross and Emily Arnold McCully

If You Lived at the Time of the American Revolution by Kay Moore

If You Were a Kid During the American Revolution by Wil Mara

If You Were There in 1776 by Barbara Brenner

Let It Begin Here! April 19, 1775: The Day the American Revolution Began by Don Brown (Actual Times)

The Midnight Ride of Flat Revere by Jeff Brown (Flat Stanley's Worldwide Adventures)

Molly Pitcher by Kirra Fedyszyn (Jr. Graphic American Legends)

Molly Pitcher: Young American Patriot by Jason Glaser (Graphic Library)

Molly Pitcher: Young Patriot by Augusta Stevenson (Childhood of Famous Americans)

Most Wanted: The Revolutionary Partnership of John Hancock and Samuel Adams by Sarah Jane Marsh

Mr. Revere and I by Robert Lawson

Mumbet's Declaration of Independence by Gretchen Woelfle

Night of Soldiers and Spies by Kate Messner (Ranger in Time)

Paul Revere's Ride by Shana Corey (Step Into Reading)

Paul Revere's Ride by Thomas Kingsley Troupe (A Fly on the Wall History)

Paul Revere's Ride by Henry Wadsworth Longfellow

Paul Revere's Ride by Xavier Niz (Graphic Library)

Phoebe the Spy by Judith Berry Griffin

The Prison-Ship Adventure of James Forten, Revolutionary War Captive by Marty Rhodes Figley (History's Kid Heroes)

Rebecca Rides for Freedom: An American Revolution Survival Story by Emma Carlson Berne (Girls Survive)

Revolutionary War on Wednesday by Mary Pope Osborne (Magic Tree House)

Sam the Minute Man by Nathaniel Benchley (I Can Read)

Samuel's Choice by Richard Berleth

The Scarlet Stockings Spy by Trinka Hakes Noble (Tales of Young Americans)

A Spy Called James: The True Story of James Lafayette, Revolutionary War Double Agent by Anne Rockwell

Sweetie by Kate Klimo (Dog Diaries)

Sybil Ludington's Midnight Ride by Marsha Amstel (On My Own History)

They Called Her Molly Pitcher by Anne Rockwell

To the Future, Ben Franklin! by Mary Pope Osborne (Magic Tree House)

Tolivar's Secret by Esther Wood Brady

Tom Jefferson: Third President of the United States by Helen Albee Monsell (Childhood of Famous Americans)

The Top-Secret Adventure of John Darragh, Revolutionary War Spy by Connie Roop (History's Kid Heroes)

A Voice of Her Own: The Story of Phillis Wheatley, Slave Poet by Kathryn Lasky (Candlewick Biographies)

We Are Patriots: Hope's Revolutionary War Diary by Kristiana Gregory (My America)

What Is the Declaration of Independence? by Michael C. Harris (Who HQ)

What's the Big Idea, Ben Franklin? by Jean Fritz

When Freedom Comes: Hope's Revolutionary War Diary by Kristiana Gregory (My America)

When Washington Crossed the Delaware: A Wintertime Story for Young Patriots by Lynne Cheney

Where Was Patrick Henry on the 29th of May? by Jean Fritz

Who Was Benedict Arnold? by James Buckley Jr. (Who HQ)

Winter at Valley Forge by Matt Doeden (Graphic Library)

You Wouldn't Want to Be at the Boston Tea Party! by Peter Cook

	The Book You Chose	**Date Completed**
22.1 Light Reader		
22.2 Interested Reader		
22.3 Avid Reader		
22.4 Committed Reader		
22.5 Enthralled Reader		

American Government

Challenge 23

Amelia Bedelia's First Vote by Herman Parish

Arthur Meets the President by Marc Brown

Bad Kitty for President by Nick Bruel

Being a Good Citizen by Sharon Coon

The Bill of Rights by Norman Pearl (American Symbols)

The Bill of Rights in Translation: What It Really Means by Amie Jane Leavitt (Fact Finders)

Class Act by Kelly Starling Lyons (Jada Jones)

The Counterfeit Constitution Mystery by Carole Marsh (Real Kids, Real Places)

The Creation of the U.S. Constitution by Michael Burgan (Graphic Library)

The Declaration of Independence by Lori Mortensen (American Symbols)

The Election Day Dilemma by Gertrude Chandler Warner (The Boxcar Children)

Everyone Counts: A Citizens' Number Book by Elissa Grodin

George Washington and the Story of the U.S. Constitution by Candice Ransom (History Speaks)

Grace for President by Kelly DiPucchio

Grace Goes to Washington by Kelly DiPucchio

The Great Seal of the United States by Norman Pearl (American Symbols)

The History of the Constitution by Lisa Trusiani (A History Book for New Readers)

How a City Works by D. J. Ward (Let's Read and Find Out)

How Not to Run for Class President by Catherine A. Hapka (Step Into Reading)

I Wonder Why Countries Fly Flags by Philip Steele

If I Ran for President by Catherine Stier

If You Were There When They Signed the Constitution by Elizabeth Levy

Marvin Redpost, Class President by Louis Sachar

Mindy Kim, Class President by Lyla Lee

A More Perfect Union: The Story of Our Constitution by Betsey Maestro and Giulio Maestro (The American Story)

The Night before Election Day by Natasha Wing

Our U.S. Capitol by Mary Firestone (American Symbols)

Pedro for President by Fran Manushkin

The President's Stuck in the Bathtub by Susan Katz

The Race Is On by Franklin W. Dixon (The Hardy Boys Secret Files)

Sabotage at Willow Woods by Carolyn Keene (Nancy Drew Diaries)

Shh! We're Writing the Constitution by Jean Fritz

Sofia Valdez, Future Prez by Andrea Beaty

So You Want to Be President? by Judith St. George

That's Not Fair! Getting to Know Your Rights and Freedoms by Danielle S. McLaughlin (CitizenKid)

The U.S. Constitution by Norman Pearl (American Symbols)

U.S. Government: What You Need to Know by Melissa Ferguson (Fact Files)

The U.S. Supreme Court by Anastasia Suen (American Symbols)

We the People: The Story of Our Constitution by Lynne Cheney

What Is a Presidential Election? by Douglas Yacka (Who HQ)

What Is Congress? by Jill Abramson (Who HQ)

What Is the Constitution? by Patricia Brennan Demuth (Who HQ)

What Is the Supreme Court? by Jill Abramson (Who HQ)

Where Is the White House? by Megan Stine (Who HQ)

The White House by Mary Firestone (American Symbols)

You and the U.S. Government by Jennifer Overend Prior

	The Book You Chose	**Date Completed**
23.1 *Light Reader*		
23.2 *Interested Reader*		
23.3 *Avid Reader*		
23.4 *Committed Reader*		
23.5 *Enthralled Reader*		

Medicine

Challenge 24

The 1918 Flu Pandemic by Katherine Krohn (Graphic Library)

All About the Flu by Megan Borgert-Spaniol (Inside Your Body)

Brave Clara Barton by Frank Murphy (Step Into Reading)

The Cheese Experiment by Geronimo Stilton

Clara Barton by Candice F. Ransom (History Maker Bios)

Clara Barton: Angel of the Battlefield by Ann Hood (The Treasure Chest)

Clara Barton: Angel of the Battlefield by Allison Lassieur (Graphic Library)

Clara Barton: The Angel of the Battlefield by Christine O'Hare (Heroes of Liberty)

Clara Barton: Founder of the American Red Cross by Augusta Stevenson (Childhood of Famous Americans)

Clara Barton: Spirit of the American Red Cross by Patricia Lakin (Ready to Read: Stories of Famous Americans)

Daisy and the Deadly Flu: A 1918 Influenza Survival Story by Julie Kathleen Gilbert (Girls Survive)

The Doctor Is In! by Megan McDonald (Judy Moody)

A Doctor like Papa by Natalie Kinsey-Warnock

Edith Cavell, Nurse Hero by Terri Arthur and Jaclyn Taylor

Elizabeth Blackwell by Elaine A. Kule (Women in Science and Technology)

Elizabeth Blackwell: Girl Doctor by Joanne Landers Henry (Childhood of Famous Americans)

Florence Nightingale by Susan Bivin Aller (History Maker Bios)

Florence Nightingale by Kitson Jazynka (DK Life Stories)

Florence Nightingale by Shelli R. Johannes (She Persisted)

Florence Nightingale by Lucy Lethbridge (Usborne)

Florence Nightingale by Shannon Zemlicka (On My Own)

Florence Nightingale: Lady with the Lamp by Trina Robbins (Graphic Library)

Frontier Surgeons: A Story about the Mayo Brothers by Emily Crofford (Creative Minds)

George's Marvelous Medicine by Roald Dahl

Germ Hunter: A Story about Louis Pasteur by Elaine Marie Alphin (Creative Minds)

Healing Warrior: A Story about Sister Elizabeth Kenny by Emily Crofford (Creative Minds)

Hero Over Here: A Story of World War I by Kathleen V. Kudlinski

High Time for Heroes by Mary Pope Osborne (Magic Tree House)

The Influenza Pandemic of 1918 by Claire O'Neal (Natural Disasters)

Jonas Salk and the Polio Vaccine by Katherine Krohn (Graphic Library)

Katie Woo Has the Flu by Fran Manushkin

Louis Pasteur and the Pasteurization by Jennifer Fandel (Graphic Library)

Maria and the Plague: A Black Death Survival Story by Natasha Bacchus-Buschkiel (Girls Survive)

Mary on Horseback: Three Mountain Stories by Rosemary Wells

Mary Seacole: Bound for the Battlefield by Susan Goldman Rubin

Medicine by Steve Parker (DK Eyewitness)

Memoir of Susie King Taylor: A Civil War Nurse by Pamela Dell

Pasteur's Fight against Microbes by Beverly Birch (Science Stories)

A Picture Book of Florence Nightingale by David A. Adler

To the Front! Clara Barton Braves the Battle of Antietam by Claudia Friddell

Understanding Viruses with Max Axiom, Super Scientist by
　　Agnieszka Biskup (Graphic Library)
Virginia Apgar by Sayantani DasGupta (She Persisted)
What Was the Plague? by Roberta Edwards (Who HQ)
Who Was Clara Barton? by Stephanie Spinner (Who HQ)
The Workers' Detective: A Story about Dr. Alice Hamilton
　　by Stephanie Sammartino McPherson (Creative Minds)

	The Book You Chose	Date Completed
24.1 *Light Reader*		
24.2 *Interested Reader*		
24.3 *Avid Reader*		
24.4 *Committed Reader*		
24.5 *Enthralled Reader*		

War of 1812

Challenge 25

An American Army of Two by Janet Greeson (On My Own History)

The Battle for St. Michaels by Emily Arnold McCully (I Can Read)

The Battle of New Orleans: The Drummer's Story by Freddi Evans

The Biggest (and Best) Flag That Ever Flew by Rebecca C. Jones

Birth of the Star-Spangled Banner by Thomas Kingsley Troupe (A Fly on the Wall History)

The Boy Who Saved the Town by Brenda Seabrooke

Caroline Takes a Chance by Kathleen Ernst (American Girl)

Caroline's Battle by Kathleen Ernst (American Girl)

Caroline's Secret Message by Kathleen Ernst (American Girl)

Changes for Caroline by Kathleen Ernst (American Girl)

Dolley Madison by Jean Patrick (History Maker Bios)

Dolley Madison Saves History by Roger Smalley (Graphic Library)

Flames in the City: A Tale of the War of 1812 by Candice Ransom (Time Spies)

Fort McHenry by Charles W. Maynard (Famous Forts Throughout American History)

Francis Scott Key's Star-Spangled Banner by Monica Kulling (Step Into Reading)

Little House by Boston Bay by Melissa Wiley (Little House: Charlotte Years)

Meet Caroline by Kathleen Ernst (American Girl)

Millie Cooper's Ride: A True Story from History by Marc Simmons

Mr. Madison's War: Causes and Effects of the War of 1812 by Kassandra Kathleen Radomski (Fact Finders)

Our Flag Was Still There: The True Story of Mary Pickersgill and the Star-Spangled Banner by Jessie Hartland

Our National Anthem by Norman Pearl (American Symbols)

A Picture Book of Dolley and James Madison by David A. Adler

A Primary Source History of the War of 1812 by John Micklos Jr. (Fact Finders)

Sisters of Scituate Light by Stephen Krensky

The Star-Spangled Banner by Nancy R. Lambert (Penguin Young Readers)

The Star-Spangled Banner by Catherine A. Welch (On My Own History)

The Star-Spangled Banner in Translation: What It Really Means by Elizabeth Raum (Fact Finders)

The Story of the Star-Spangled Banner by Ryan Jacobson (Graphic Library)

The Town That Fooled the British: A War of 1812 Story by Lisa Papp (Tales of Young Americans)

The Traveler's Tricks: A Caroline Mystery by Laurie Calkhoven (American Girl)

The War of 1812 by Kevin Cunningham (Expansion of Our Nation)

The War of 1812: By the Dawn's Early Light by Heather E. Schwartz

Washington Is Burning by Marty Rhodes Figley (On My Own History)

	The Book You Chose	Date Completed
25.1 *Light Reader*		
25.2 *Interested Reader*		
25.3 *Avid Reader*		
25.4 *Committed Reader*		
25.5 *Enthralled Reader*		

Australia

Challenge 26

20 Fun Facts about the Great Barrier Reef by Emily Mahoney (Fun Fact File)

The Alice Stories: Our Australian Girl by Davina Bell

Aqua Dog Flames by Lisa Van Der Wielen

Are We There Yet? by Alison Lester

Audrey of the Outback by Christine Harris

An Aussie Year: Twelve Months in the Life of Australian Kids by Tania McCartney

Australia by Anita Ganeri (Country Guides with Benjamin Blog)

Australia by Mary Lindeen (Continents of the World)

Australia by Sean McCollom (Country Explorers)

Australia by Sarah Tieck (Explore the Countries)

Australia by Shalini Vallepur (Welcome to My World)

The Australian Boomerang Bonanza by Jeff Brown (Flat Stanley's Worldwide Adventures)

Australia's Pink Lakes by Patricia Hutchison (Nature's Mysteries)

Baby Kangaroos by Megan Bogert-Spaniol (Blastoff Readers: Super Cute!)

Baby Koalas by Megan Bogert-Spaniol (Blastoff Readers: Super Cute!)

Bindi Irwin's Wild Life by Emily Klein

Bob the Railway Dog by Corinne Fenton

Cultural Traditions in Australia by Molly Aloian

D Is for Down Under: An Australia Alphabet by Devin Scillian

Diary of a Wombat by Jackie French

Dingoes at Dinnertime by Mary Pope Osborne (Magic Tree House)

Down and Out Down Under by Geronimo Stilton

Down Under by Jan Reynolds (Vanishing Cultures)

Expedition Down Under by Rebecca Carmi (The Magic School Bus Chapter Book)

Explore Australia by Vernonica B. Wilkins (A Look at Continents)

The Firebird Rocket by Franklin W. Dixon (Hardy Boys)

G'Day, Australia! by April Pulley Sayre (Our Amazing Continents)

I Escaped the Prison Island by Juliet Fry and Scott Peters

Indigenous Australian Cultures by Mary Colson (Global Cultures)

Introducing Australia by Anita Ganeri (Introducing Continents)

Jimmy the Joey: The True Story of an Amazing Koala Rescue by Deborah Lee Rose and Susan Kelly (National Geographic Kids)

Kangaroos by Kari Schuetz (Blastoff Readers: Animal Safari)

A Kid's Guide to Australia by Jack L. Roberts and Michael Owens

Kira's Animal Rescue by Erin Teagan (American Girl)

Kira Down Under by Erin Teagan (American Girl)

Koalas by Kari Schuetz (Blastoff Readers: Animal Safari)

The Letty Books: Our Australian Girl by Alison Lloyd

Look What Came from Australia by Kevin Davis

Meet Our New Student from Australia by Ann Weil

Mirror by Jeannie Baker

The Mystery at the Coral Reef by Harper Paris (Greetings from Somewhere)

Mystery of the Min Min Lights by Janelle Diller (Pack-n-Go Girls)

Mystery of the Rusty Key by Janelle Diller (Pack-n-Go Girls)

The Mystery on the Great Barrier Reef by Carole Marsh (Around the World in 80 Mysteries)

Never Box With a Kangeroo by Nancy Krulik (Magic Bone)

Outback All–Stars by Kristin Earhart (Race the Wild)

The Pearlie Stories: Our Australian Girl by Gabrielle Want

The Plunder Down Under by James Patterson (Treasure Hunters)

Sand Swimmers: The Secret Life of Australia's Desert Wilderness by Narelle Oliver

The Secret World of Wombats by Jackie French

Snake and Lizard by Joy Cowley

Snappy Crocodile Tale by Niki Foreman (DK Readers)

Spotlight on Australia by Bobbie Kalman (Spotlight on My Country)

Stoat on Stage by Jennifer Gray (The Travels of Ermine)

Thea Stilton and the Mountain of Fire by Thea Stilton

This Is Australia by M. Sasek

Welcome to Australia by Mary Berendes (Welcome to the World)

Welcome, Wombat by Kama Einhorn (True Tales of Rescue)

Where Is the Great Barrier Reef? by Nico Medina (Who HQ)

Wombats by Margo Gates (Blastoff Readers: Animal Safari)

You Wouldn't Want to Be a Convict Sent to Australia! by Meredith Costain

The Book You Chose	**Date Completed**
26.1 *Light Reader*		
26.2 *Interested Reader*		
26.3 *Avid Reader*		
26.4 *Committed Reader*		
26.5 *Enthralled Reader*		

American Symbols / Landmarks

Challenge 27

American Symbols: What You Need to Know by Melissa Ferguson (Fact Files)

Betsy Ross and the American Flag by Kay Melchisedech Olson (Graphic Library)

Betsy Ross and the Silver Thimble by Stephanie Greene (Ready to Read: Childhood of Famous Americans)

Betsy Ross: Designer of Our Flag by Ann Well (Childhood of Famous Americans)

Betsy Ross: The Story of Our Flag by Pamela Chanko (Easy Reader Biographies)

Betsy Ross's Star by Stacia Deutsch (Blast to the Past)

A Capitol Crime by Carolyn Keene (Nancy Drew Diaries)

The Copper Lady by Alice and Kent Ross (On My Own History)

Challenger: America's Favorite Eagle by Margot Theis Raven

Flags over America by Cheryl Harness

For Spacious Skies: Katharine Lee Bates and the Inspiration for "America the Beautiful" by Nancy Churnin

I Pledge Allegiance by June Swanson (On My Own)

The Journey of the One and Only Declaration of Independence by Judith St. George

The Madcap Mystery of the Missing Liberty Bell by Carole Marsh (Real Kids, Real Places)

Message in the Mountain by Candice Ransom (Time Spies)

The Monumental Mystery on the National Mall by Carole Marsh (Real Kids, Real Places)

Mount Rushmore: Myths, Legends, and Facts by Jessica Gunderson (Fact Finders)

Mount Rushmore's Hidden Room and Other Monumental Secrets by Laurie Calkhoven (Ready to Read: Secrets of American History)

The Mystery at Mount Rushmore by Carole Marsh (Real Kids, Real Places)

The Mystery at Mount Vernon by Carole Marsh (Real Kids, Real Places)

The Mystery at Yellowstone National Park by Carole Marsh (Real Kids, Real Places)

O, Say Can You See? America's Symbols, Landmarks, and Important Words by Sheila Keenan

One Nation: America by the Numbers by Devin Scillian

Our 50 States: A Family Adventure across America by Lynne Cheney

Our American Symbols series by Lisa Bullard

Red, White, and Blue: The Story of the American Flag by John Herman (Penguin Young Readers)

Red, White, Blue, and Uncle Who? The Stories behind Some of America's Patriotic Symbols by Teresa Bateman

Saving the Liberty Bell by Marty Rhodes Figley (On My Own History)

Secrets of the American History: Mount Rushmore's Hidden Room and Other Monumental Secrets by Laurie Calkhoven (Ready to Read)

The Statue of Liberty by Nancy Ohlin (Blast Back)

The Statue of Liberty by Lucille Recht Penner (Step Into Reading)

The Story of the Statue of Liberty by Xavier W. Niz (Graphic Library)

The U.S. Capital Commotion by Jeff Brown (Flat Stanley's Worldwide Adventures)

What Are You Figuring Now? A Story about Benjamin Banneker by Jeri Ferris (Creative Minds Biography)

What Is the Statue of Liberty by Joan Holub (Who HQ)

Where Is Mount Rushmore? by True Kelley (Who HQ)

Who Was Betsy Ross? by James Buckley Jr. (Who HQ)

You Wouldn't Want to Be a Worker on the Statue of Liberty! by John Malam

	The Book You Chose	Date Completed
27.1 Light Reader		
27.2 Interested Reader		
27.3 Avid Reader		
27.4 Committed Reader		
27.5 Enthralled Reader		

American Trailblazers

Challenge 28

The Adventures of Lewis and Clark by John Bakeless (Dover Children's Classics)

The Back of Beyond: A Story about Lewis and Clark by Andy Russell Bowen (Creative Minds)

Bold Riders: The Story of the Pony Express by John Micklos Jr. (Fact Findeers: Adventures on the American Frontier)

Cutting a Path: Daniel Boonen and the Cumberland Gap by Elizabeth Raum (Fact Finders: Adventures on the American Frontier)

Daniel Boone by John Bakeless (Classics Illustrated)

Daniel Boone by Candice F. Ransom (History Maker Bios)

Daniel Boone by Thomas Streissguth (On My Own)

Daniel Boone: Young Hunter and Tracker by Augusta Stevenson (Childhood of Famous Americans)

Explorers of North America by Christine Taylor-Butler (A True Book: American History)

Exploring with the Lewis and Clark Expedition by Jessica Rusick (This or That? History Edition)

Folks Call Me Appleseed John by Andrew Glass

How We Crossed the West: The Adventures of Lewis and Clark by Rosalyn Schanzer (National Geographic)

I Am Sacagawea by Grace Norwich

Into the West: Causes and Effects of U.S. Westward Expansion by Terry Collins (Fact Finders: Cause and Effect)

Jim Bridger's Alarm Clock and Other Tall Tales by Sid Fleischman

John Chapman: The Man Who Was Johnny Appleseed by Carol Greene (Rookie Biography)

Johnny Appleseed by Andrea P. Smith (Jr. Graphic American Legends)

Johnny Appleseed: An American Who Made a Difference by Alyse Sweeney (Easy Reader Biographies)

The Journey of York: The Unsung Hero of the Lewis and Clark Expedition by Hasan Davis

Kit Carson and the Wild Frontier by Ralph Moody

The Legend of Johnny Appleseed by Martin Powell (Graphic Spin)

Lewis and Clark by Candice F. Ransom (History Makers Bios)

Lewis and Clark: A Prairie Dog for the President by Shirley Raye Redmond (Step Into Reading)

The Lewis and Clark Expedition by Jessica Gunderson (Graphic Library)

The Lewis and Clark Expedition by Blythe Lawrence (Expansion of Our Nation)

The Lewis and Clark Expedition by John Perritano (A True Book)

Lewis and Clark: Explorers of the American West by Steven Kroll

Lewis and Clark for Kids: Their Journey of Discovery by Janis Herbert

A Picture Book of Daniel Boone by David A. Adler

A Picture Book of Lewis and Clark by David A. Adler

A Picture Book of Sacagawea by David A. Adler

A Primary Source History of Westward Expansion by Steven Otfinoski (Fact Finders)

A Right Fine Life: Kit Carson on the Santa Fe Trail by Andrew Glass

Sacagawea by Liselotte Erdrich

Sacagawea by Kitson Jazynka (National Geographic Kids)

Sacagawea by Jane Sutcliffe (History Maker Bios)

Sacagawea: American Pathfinder by Flora Warren Seymour (Childhood of Famous Americans)

Sacagawea: Courageous Trailblazer! by James Buckley (Show Me History)

Sacagawea: Journey Into the West by Jessica S. Gunderson (Graphic Library)

Sacagawea's Strength by Stacia Deutsch and Rhody Cohon (Blast to the Past)

Sacajawea: Her True Story by Joyce Milton (Penguin Young Readers)

Seaman: The Dog Who Explored the West with Lewis and Clark by Gail Langer Karwoski

The Trailblazing Life of Daniel Boone and How Early Americans Took to the Road by Cheryl Harness (National Geographic)

What Was the Lewis and Clark Expedition? by Judith St. George (Who HQ)

What Was the Wild West? by Janet B. Pascal (Who HQ)

Who Was Daniel Boone? by Sydelle Kramer (Who HQ)

Who Was Johnny Appleseed? by Joan Holub (Who HQ)

Who Was Sacagawea? by Judith Bloom Fradin and Dennis Brindell Fradin (Who HQ)

The Wild West by Andrew Langley (100 Facts)

You Wouldn't Want to Explore with Lewis and Clark! by Jacqueline Morley

Your Life as a Private on the Lewis and Clark Expedition by Jessica Gunderson (The Way It Was)

	The Book You Chose	**Date Completed**
28.1 Light Reader		
28.2 Interested Reader		
28.3 Avid Reader		
28.4 Committed Reader		
28.5 Enthralled Reader		

Pirates

Challenge 29

100 Facts on Pirates by Andrew Langley

Captain Stone's Revenge by Carolyn Keene (Nancy Drew Diaries)

Double Take by Carolyn Keene (Nancy Drew and the Clue Crew)

The Golden Age of Pirates: An Interactive History Adventure by Bob Temple (You Choose)

The Happy Hollisters at Sea Gull Beach by Jerry West

The Hurricane Mystery by Gertrude Chandler Warner (The Boxcar Children)

I Escaped Pirates in the Caribbean by Ellie Crowe and Scott Peters

Jean Lafitte: The Pirate Who Saved America by Susan Goldman Rubin

The Mystery of Blackbeard the Pirate by Carole Marsh (Real Kids, Real Places)

The Mystery of the Pirate Ship by Geronimo Stilton

The Mystery of the Pirate's Map by Gertrude Chandler Warner (The Boxcar Children)

The Mystery of the Pirate's Treasure by Penny Warner (The Code Busters Club)

Mystery on Skull Island by Elizabeth McDavid Jones (Mysteries Through History)

P Is for Pirate: A Pirate Alphabet by Eve Bunting

The Peril of the Pirate's Curse by Leah Cupps (Harley James)

Pirate by Richard Platt (DK Eyewitness)

The Pirate Captain by Terry Deary (Pirate Tales)

Pirate Diary: The Journal of Jake Carpenter by Richard Platt (Historical Diaries)

The Pirate Ghost by Franklin W. Dixon (Hardy Boys Clue Book)

Pirate Island Adventure by Peggy Parish

The Pirate Prisoner by Terry Deary (Pirate Tales)

The Pirate Queen by Terry Deary (Pirate Tales)

Pirate Ship: Explore the Golden Age of Piracy by Paul Beck (Inside Out)

The Pirate Treasure by Zander Bingham (Jack Jones)

Pirates by Mary Pope Osborne (Magic Tree House Fact Tracker)

Pirates on the Bay by Steven K. Smith (The Virginia Mysteries)

Pirates Past Noon by Mary Pope Osborne (Magic Tree House)

Pocket Pirates series by Chris Mould

Puppy Pirates series by Erin Soderberg

Salty Dog by Brad Strickland (The Adventures of Wishbone)

The Secret of Pirates' Hill by Franklin W. Dixon (The Hardy Boys)

Shipwreck on the Pirate Islands by Geronimo Stilton

Treasure Island by Robert Louis Stevenson, adapted by Deidre S. Laiken (Great Illustrated Classics)

Treasure Island by Robert Louis Stevenson, adapted by Lisa Norby (Stepping Stones)

Treasure Island retold from the Robert Louis Stevenson original (Classic Starts)

Treasure Trouble by Carolyn Keene (Nancy Drew Clue Crew)

Who Was Blackbeard? by James Buckley Jr. (Who HQ)

You Wouldn't Want to Be a Pirate's Prisoner by John Malam

The Book You Chose	**Date Completed**
29.1 _Light Reader_	
29.2 _Interested Reader_	
29.3 _Avid Reader_	
29.4 _Committed Reader_	
29.5 _Enthralled Reader_	

South America

Challenge 30

Ada's Violin: The Story of the Recycled Orchestra of Paraguay by Susan Hood

Afternoon on the Amazon by Mary Pope Osborne (Magic Tree House)

Along the Tapajos by Fernando Vilela

The Amazon (DK Eyewitness)

Amazon Fever by Kathleen Weidner Zoehfeld

Argentina by Kari Schuetz (Blastoff Readers: Exploring Countries)

Argentina by Kristine Spanier (All Around the World)

The Best Tailor in Pinbaue by Eymard Toledo

Blinded by the Shining Path: Rómulo Sauñe by Dave and Neta Jackson (Trailblazer Books)

Bolivia by Lisa Owings (Blastoff Readers: Exploring Countries)

Brazil by Joanne Mattern (All Around the World)

Brazil by Colleen Sexton (Blastoff Readers: Exploring Countries)

Chile by Lisa Owings (Blastoff Readers: Exploring Countries)

Chile by Kristine Spanier (All Around the World)

Colombia by Walter Simmons (Blastoff Readers: Exploring Countries)

Cultural Traditions in Argentina by Adrianna Morganelli

Cultural Traditions in Brazil by Molly Aloian

Ecuador by Joanne Mattern (All Around the World)

Ecuador by Lisa Owings (Blastoff Readers: Exploring Countries)

From My Window by Otavio Junior

I Escaped Amazon River Pirates by Scott Peters

The Khipu and the Final Key by Gertrude Chandler Warner (The Boxcar Children)

Late Lunch with Llamas by Mary Pope Osborne (Magic Tree House)

Lea Dives In by Lisa Yee (American Girl)

Lea Leads the Way by Lisa Yee (American Girl)

Let's Visit Machu Picchu! by Lisa Manzione (The Adventures of Bella and Harry)

Let's Visit Rio de Janeiro! by Lisa Manzione (The Adventures of Bella and Harry)

Life in the Amazon Rainforest by Ginjer L. Clarke (Penguin Young Readers)

Llamas by Laura Buller (DK Readers)

Lola Levine and the Vacation Dream by Monica Brown

Lost in the Amazon: A Battle for Survival in the Heart of the Rainforest by Tod Olson

The Mystery across the Secret Bridge by Harper Paris (Greetings from Somewhere)

The Mystery at Machu Picchu by Carole Marsh (Around the World in 80 Mysteries)

The Mystery in the Amazon Rainforest by Carole Marsh (Around the World in 80 Mysteries)

Mystery of the Lazy Loggerhead by Lisa Travis (Pack-n-Go Girls)

Mystery of the Troubled Toucan by Lisa Travis (Pack-n-Go Girls)

Peru by Lisa Owings (Blastoff Readers: Exploring Countries)

A Picture Book of Simón Bolívar by David A. Adler

Rain Forest Explorer by Rupert Matthews (DK Readers)

Rain Forest Relay by Kristin Earhart (Race the Wild)

Rumble in the Jungle by Geronimo Stilton

Secret of the Andes by Ann Nolan Clark

Take Your Time: A Tale of Harriet, the Galapagos Tortoise by Eva Furrow and Donna Jo Napoli

Terror on the Amazon: The Quest for El Dorado by Phil Gates (DK Readers)

Thea Stilton and the Chocolate Sabotage by Thea Stilton
Thea Stilton and the Race for Gold by Thea Stilton
Thea Stilton and the Secret City by Thea Stilton
Tuki and Moka: A Tale of Two Tamarins by Judy Young (Tales of the World)
Uruguay by Emily Rose Oachs (Blastoff Readers: Exploring Countries)
Venezuela by Kari Schuetz (Blastoff Readers: Exploring Countries)

What's Up in the Amazon Rainforest by Ginjer L. Clarke
Where Are the Galapagos Islands? by Megan Stine (Who HQ)
Where Is Machu Picchu? by Megan Stine (Who HQ)
Where Is the Amazon? by Sarah Fabiny (Who HQ)
Your Passport to Argentina by Nancy Dickmann
Your Passport to Ecuador by Sarah Cords
Your Passport to Peru by Ryan Gale

	The Book You Chose	**Date Completed**
30.1 Light Reader		
30.2 Interested Reader		
30.3 Avid Reader		
30.4 Committed Reader		
30.5 Enthralled Reader		

Slavery / Underground Railroad

Challenge 31

Addy: A New Beginning by Denise Lewis Patrick (American Girl)

Addy: Finding Freedom by Connie Porter (American Girl)

Allen Jay and the Underground Railroad by Marlene Targ Brill (On My Own History)

Ann Fights for Freedom: An Underground Railroad Survival Story by Nikki Shannon Smith (Girls Survive)

Bell's Star by Alison Hart (Horse Diaries)

Bound for America: The Forced Migration of Africans to the New World by James Haskins

Christmas in the Big House, Christmas in the Quarters by Patricia and Fredrick McKissack

The Daring Escape of Ellen Craft by Cathy Moore (On My Own History)

Dear Benjamin Banneker by Andrea Davis Pinkney

Eliza's Freedom Road: An Underground Railroad Diary by Jerdine Nolen

Ellen Craft's Escape from Slavery by Cathy Moore (History Speaks)

Escape From Slavery: Five Journeys to Freedom by Doreen Rappaport

Escape North! The Story of Harriet Tubman (Step Into Reading)

The Escape of Oney Judge: Martha Washington's Slave Finds Freedom by Emily Arnold McCully

Escape South by Kim L. Siegelson (Stepping Stones)

Flying Free: Corey's Underground Railroad Diary by Sharon Dennis Wyeth (My America)

Freedom from Slavery: Causes and Effects of the Emancipation Proclamation by Brianna Hall (Fact Finders)

Freedom's School by Lesa Cline-Ransome

Freedom's Wings: Corey's Underground Railroad Diary by Sharon Dennis Wyeth (My America)

Friend on Freedom River by Gloria Whelan (Tales of Young Americans)

From Slave to Soldier: Based on a True Civil War Story by Deborah Hopkinson (Ready to Read)

Go Free or Die: A Story about Harriet Tubman by Jeri Ferris (Creative Minds)

Harriet Tubman by Andrea Davis Pinkney (She Persisted)

Harriet Tubman by Maryann N. Weidt (History Maker Bios)

Harriet Tubman and the Freedom Train by Sharon Gayle (Ready to Read: Stories of Famous Americans)

Harriet Tubman and the Underground Railroad by Michael J. Martin (Graphic Library)

Harriet Tubman: Fighter for Freedom! by James Buckley Jr. (Show Me History)

Harriet Tubman: Follow the North Star by Violet Findley (Easy Reader Biographies)

Henry's Freedom Box by Ellen Levine

If You Lived When There Was Slavery in America by Anne Kamma

If You Traveled on the Underground Railroad by Ellen Levine

The Listeners by Gloria Whelan (Tales of Young Americans)

Long Road to Freedom by Kate Messner (Ranger in Time)

Message in the Sky: Corey's Underground Railroad Diary by Sharon Dennis Wyeth (My America)

The Mystery on the Underground Railroad by Carole Marsh (Real Kids, Real Places)

A Picture Book of Frederick Douglass by David A. Adler

A Picture Book of Harriet Beecher Stowe by David A. Adler

A Picture Book of Harriet Tubman by David A. Adler

A Picture Book of Sojourner Truth by David A. Adler

President of the Underground Railroad: A Story about Levi Coffin by Gwenyth Swain (Creative Minds)

A Primary Source History of Slavery in the United States by Allison Crotzer Kimmel (Fact Finders)

Prisoner for Liberty by Marty Rhodes Figley (On My Own History)

Secrets of American History: Heroes Who Risked Everything for Freedom by Patricia Lakin (Ready to Read)

Seeking Freedom: The Untold Story of Fortress Monroe and the Ending of Slavery in America by Selene Castrovilla

Sojourner Truth: Path to Glory by Peter Merchant (Ready to Read: Stories of Famous Americans)

The Story of Harriet Tubman by Christine Platt (A Biography Book for New Readers)

Tennessee Rose by Jane Kendall (Horse Diaries)

The Underground Railroad by Bonnie Bader (American Girl: Real Stories From My Time)

The Underground Railroad Adventure of Allen Jay, Antislavery Activist by Marlene Targ Brill (History's Kid Heroes)

The Underground Railroad: An Interactive History Adventure by Allison Lassieur (You Choose)

Underground to Canada by Barbara Smucker

Unspoken: A Story from the Underground Railroad by Henry Cole

Voice of Freedom: A Story about Frederick Douglass by Maryann N. Weidt (Creative Minds)

Walking the Road to Freedom: A Story about Sojourner Truth by Jeri Ferris (Creative Minds)

What Was the Underground Railroad? by Yona Zeldis McDonough (Who HQ)

Who Was Frederick Douglass? by April Jones Prince (Who HQ)

Who Was Harriet Beecher Stowe? by Dana Meachen Rau (Who HQ)

Who Was Harriet Tubman? by Yona Zeldis McDonough (Who HQ)

Who Was Sojourner Truth? by Yona Zeldis McDonough (Who HQ)

	The Book You Chose	Date Completed
31.1 Light Reader		
31.2 Interested Reader		
31.3 Avid Reader		
31.4 Committed Reader		
31.5 Enthralled Reader		

Pioneers / Settlers

Challenge 32

Annie Oakley by Sandra J. Hiller (Jr. Graphic American Legends)

Annie Oakley by Ginger Wadsworth (History Maker Bios)

Annie Oakley: Young Markswoman by Ellen Wilson (Childhood of Famous Americans)

As Far As I Can See: Meg's Prairie Diary by Kate McMullan (My America)

A Book for Black-Eyed Susan by Judy Young (Tales of Young Americans)

Bronco Charlie and the Pony Express by Marlene Targ Brill (On My Own History)

Buffalo Bill by Ingri and Edgar Parin d'Aulaire

Buffalo Bill and the Pony Express by Eleanor Coerr (I Can Read)

Buffalo Bill: Frontier Daredevil by Augusta Stevenson (Childhood of Famous Americans)

Buffalo Soldiers and the American West by Jason Glaser (Graphic Library)

Clara Morgan and the Oregon Trail Journey by Marty Rhodes Figley (History Speaks)

Clouds of Terror by Catherine A. Welch (On My Own)

Daily Life in a Covered Wagon by Paul Erickson

Daniel's Duck by Clyde Robert Bulla (I Can Read)

Davy Crockett by Elaine Marie Alphin (History Maker Bios)

Davy Crockett by Lou Cameron (Classics Illustrated)

Davy Crockett by Andrea P. Smith (Jr. Graphic American Legends)

Davy Crockett: A Life on the Frontier by Stephen Krensky (Ready to Read: Stories of Famous Americans)

Davy Crockett: Young Rifleman by Aileen Wells Parks (Childhood of Famous Americans)

Don't Know Much about the Pioneers by Kenneth C. Davis

Enduring the Oregon Trail by Jessica Rusick (This or That? History Edition)

Facing West: A Story of the Oregon Trail by Kathleen V. Kudlinski (Once Upon America)

A Fine Start: Meg's Prairie Diary by Kate McMullan (My America)

For This Land: Meg's Prairie Diary by Kate McMullan (My America)

Hope's Path to Glory: The Story of a Family's Journey on the Overland Trail by Jerdine Nolen

I Survived the Children's Blizzard, 1888 by Lauren Tarshis

If You Traveled West in a Covered Wagon by Ellen Levine

If You Were a Kid on the Oregon Trail by Josh Gregory

If You Were a Pioneer on the Prairie by Anne Kamma

If You Were Me and Lived in the American West by Carole P. Roman

John Deere by Jane Sutcliffe (History Maker Bios)

The Josefina Story Quilt by Eleanor Coerr (I Can Read)

Journey of a Pioneer by Patricia J. Murphy (DK Readers)

Koda by Patricia Hermes (Horse Diaries)

Little House on the Prairie series by Laura Ingalls Wilder

Minnow and Rose: An Oregon Trail Story by Judy Young (Tales of Young Americans)

The Mystery on the Oregon Trail by Carole Marsh (Real Kids, Real Places)

Next Spring an Oriole by Gloria Whelan (Stepping Stones)

The Oregon Trail: An Interactive History Adventure by Matt Doeden (You Choose)

A Perfect Place: Joshua's Oregon Trail Diary by Patricia Hermes (My America)

A Picture Book of Davy Crockett by David A. Adler

Pioneer Cat by William H. Hooks (Stepping Stones)

Pioneer Plowmaker: A Story about John Deere by David R. Collins (Creative Minds)

The Prairie Adventure of Sarah and Annie, Blizzard Survivors by Marty Rhodes Figley (History's Kid Heroes)

Rescue on the Oregon Trail by Kate Messner (Ranger in Time)

Riding the Pony Express by Clyde Robert Bulla

Roughing It on the Oregon Trail by Diane Stanley (The Time-Traveling Twins)

The Rough-Riding Adventure of Bronco Charlie, Pony Express Rider by Marlene Targ Brill (History's Kid Heroes)

Sarah Journeys West: An Oregon Trail Survival Story by Nikki Shannon Smith (Girls Survive)

The Schoolchildren's Blizzard by Marty Rhodes Figley (On My Own History)

Surviving the Journey: The Story of the Oregon Trail by Danny Kravitz (Fact Finders)

Surviving the Santa Fe Trail by Jessica Rusick (This or That? History Edition)

The Sweetwater Run: The Story of Buffalo Bill Cody and the Pony Express by Andrew Glass

Twister on Tuesday by Mary Pope Osborne (Magic Tree House)

Wagon Train by Sydelle Kramer (Penguin Young Readers)

Westward to Home: Joshua's Oregon Trail Diaries by Patricia Hermes (My America)

Who Was Annie Oakley? by Stephanie Spinner (Who HQ)

Who Was Davy Crockett? by Gail Herman (Who HQ)

Who Was Laura Ingalls Wilder? by Patricia Brennan Demuth (Who HQ)

Wild West by Mary Pope Osborne (Magic Tree House)

A Wild Year: Joshua's Oregon Trail Diary by Patricia Hermes (My America)

With Open Hands: A Story about Biddy Mason by Jeri Chase Ferris (Creative Minds)

Working on the Pony Express by Jessica Rusick (This or That? History Edition)

You Wouldn't Want to Be a Pony Express Rider! by Thomas Ratliff

You Wouldn't Want to Be an American Pioneer! by Jacqueline Morley

You Wouldn't Want to Live in a Wild West Town! by Peter Hicks

Your Life as a Pioneer on the Oregon Trail by Jessica Gunderson (The Way It Was)

	The Book You Chose	**Date Completed**
32.1 Light Reader		
32.2 Interested Reader		
32.3 Avid Reader		
32.4 Committed Reader		
32.5 Enthralled Reader		

Native Americans

Challenge 33

Ahyoka and the Talking Leaves by Peter and Connie Roop

Apache Resistance: Causes and Effects of Geronimo's Campaign by Pamela Jain Dell (Fact Finders)

Black Elk's Vision: A Lakota Story by S.D. Nelson

The Boy Who Lived with the Bears and Other Iroquois Stories by Joseph Bruchac

Buffalo before Breakfast by Mary Pope Osborne (Magic Tree House)

Buffalo Song by Joseph Bruchac

Chief Joseph by Jane Sutcliffe (History Maker Bios)

Children of the Long House by Joseph Bruchac

Crazy Horse: Brave Warrior by Ann Hood (The Treasure Chest)

Crazy Horse: Young War Chief by George E. Stanley (Childhood of Famous Americans)

Crazy Horse's Vision by Joseph Bruchac

D Is for Drum: A Native American Alphabet by Michael Shoulders

Defending the Land: Causes and Effects of Red Cloud's War by Nadia Higgins (Fact Finders)

Don't Know Much about Sitting Bull by Kenneth C. Davis

The Earth under Sky Bear's Feet: Native American Poems of the Land by Joseph Bruchac

Forced Removal: Causes and Effects of the Trail of Tears by Heather E. Schwartz (Fact Finders)

Geronimo by Catherine A. Welch (History Maker Bios)

Geronimo: Young Warrior by George E. Stanley (Childhood of Famous Americans)

Golden Sun by Whitney Sanderson (Horse Diaries)

Hiawatha and the Peacemaker by Robbie Robertson

If You Lived with the Cherokees by Anna Kamma, Connie Roop, and Peter Roop

If You Lived with the Iroquois by Ellen Levine

If You Lived with the Sioux Indians by Ann McGovern

The Indian Removal Act and the Trail of Tears by Susan E. Hamen (Expansion of Our Nation)

Kaya series by Janet Beeler Shaw (American Girl)

Last Battle: Causes and Effects of the Massacre at Wounded Knee by Pamela Jain Dell (Fact Finders)

The Last of the Mohicans by James Fenimore Cooper, adapted by Les Martin (Stepping Stones)

Last Stand: Causes and Effects of the Battle of Little Bighorn by Nadia Higgins (Fact Finders)

Living with the Senecas: A Story about Mary Jemison by Susan Bivin Aller (Creative Minds)

Many Nations: An Alphabet of Native America by Joseph Bruchac

Mary and the Trail of Tears: A Cherokee Removal Survival Story by Andrea L. Rogers (Girls Survive)

Native American Homes: From Longhouses to Wigwams by P. V. Knight (Native American Cultures)

Navajo Long Walk: The Tragic Story of a Proud Peoples' Forced March from Their Homeland by Joseph Bruchac (National Geographic)

Naya Nuki: Shoshoni Girl Who Ran by Kenneth Thomasma

Night of the Full Moon by Gloria Whelan (Stepping Stones)

North American Indian by David Murdoch (DK Eyewitness)

North American Indian Tales by W. T. Larned (Dover Children's Thrift Classics)

North American Indians by Marie and Douglas Gorsline

Om-Kas-Toe: Blackfeet Twin Captures an Elkdog by Kenneth Thomasma

Pathki Nana: Kootenai Girl Solves a Mystery by Kenneth Thomasma

People of the Breaking Day by Marcia Sewall

A Picture Book of Sitting Bull by David A. Adler

Red Cloud: A Lakota Story of War and Surrender by S.D. Nelson

Quanah Parker by Shannon Zemlicka (History Maker Bios)

Seasons of the Circle: A Native American Year by Joseph Bruchac

Seeking Freedom: Causes and Effects of the Flight of the Nez Perce by Heather E. Schwartz (Fact Finders)

Seneca Chief, Army General: A Story about Ely Parker by Elizabeth Van Steenwyk (Creative Minds)

Sequoyah by Laura Hamilton Waxman (History Maker Bios)

Shadow of the Wolf by Gloria Whelan (Stepping Stones)

Sitting Bull by Susan Bivin Aller (History Maker Bios)

Sitting Bull by Lucille Recht Penner (Penguin Young Readers)

Sitting Bull: Dakota Boy by Augusta Stevenson (Childhood of Famous Americans)

Sitting Bull: Lakota Warrior and Defender of His People by S.D. Nelson

Soun Tetoken: Nez Perce Boy Tames a Stallion by Kenneth Thomasma

Tecumseh by Susan Bivin Aller (History Maker Bios)

Thirteen Moons on Turtle's Back: A Native American Year of Moons by Joseph Bruchac

Thomas Jefferson and the Ghostriders by Howard Goldsmith (Ready to Read)

Thunder Rolling in the Mountains by Scott O'Dell

The Trail of Tears by Joseph Bruchac (Step Into Reading)

Voice of the Poiutes: A Story about Sarah Winnemucca by Jodie Shull (Creative Minds)

Who Was Sitting Bull? by Stephanie Spinner (Who HQ)

	The Book You Chose	Date Completed
33.1 Light Reader		
33.2 Interested Reader		
33.3 Avid Reader		
33.4 Committed Reader		
33.5 Enthralled Reader		

Texas/Mexico

Challenge 34

Adelita: A Mexican Cinderella Story by Tomie dePaola

The Alamo by Kristin L. Nelson(Lightning Bolt)

Alamo All-Stars by Nathan Hale (Hazardous Tales)

The Alamo: Myths, Legends, and Facts by Jessica Gunderson (Fact Finders)

The Amazing Mexican Secret by Jeff Brown (Flat Stanley's Worldwide Adventures)

Basil in Mexico by Eve Titus (The Great Mouse Detective)

The Battle of the Alamo by Matt Doeden (Graphic Library)

The Battle of the Alamo: An Interactive History Adventure by Amie Jane Leavitt (You Choose)

Cactus Soup by Eric A. Kimmel

Cinco de Mayo by Linda Lowery (On My Own)

Domitila: A Cinderella Tale from the Mexican Tradition by Jewell Reinhart Coburn

Enrique Esparza and the Battle of the Alamo by Susan Taylor Brown (History Speaks)

The Happy Hollisters and the Mystery of the Mexican Idol by Jerry West

Hill of Fire by Thomas P. Lewis (I Can Read)

How to Get Rich on a Texas Cattle Drive: In Which I Tell theHonest Truth about Rampaging Rustlers, Stampeding Steers and Other Fateful Hazards on the Wild Chisholm Trail by Tod Olson

Juneteenth by Vaunda Micheaux Nelson and Drew Nelson (On My Own Holidays)

Juneteenth Jamboree by Carole Boston Weatherford

A Kid's Guide to Mexico by Jack L. Roberts

L Is for Lone Star: A Texas Alphabet by Carol Crane

Let's Look at Mexico by A. M. Reynolds (Let's Look at Countries)

Make Way for Sam Houston by Jean Fritz

The Mexican-American War by Nick Rebman (Expansion of Our Nation)

Mexico by Colleen Sexton (Blastoff Readers: Exploring Countries)

The Mystery at the Alamo by Gertrude Chandler Warner (The Boxcar Children)

The Mystery of the Alamo Ghost by Carole Marsha (Real Kids, Real Places)

Mystery of the Disappearing Dolphin by Janelle Diller (Pack-n-Go Girls)

Mystery of the Thief in the Night by Janelle Diller (Pack-n-Go Girls)

Next Stop: Mexico by Ginger McDonnell

P Is for Piñata: A Mexico Alphabet by Tony Johnston

A Picture Book of Sam Houston by David A. Adler

Sam Houston: A Fearless Statesman by Joanne Mattern

Sam Houston: Standing Firm by Mary Dodson Wade

Shadow of the Shark by Mary Pope Osborne (Magic Tree House)

Showdown at the Alamo by Jeff Brown (Flat Stanley's Worldwide Adventures)

Soccer on Sunday by Mary Pope Osborne (Magic Tree House)

The Story of Juneteeth: An Interactive History Adventure by Steven Otfinoski (You Choose)

Susanna of the Alamo by John Jakes

Texas by Mary Pope Osborne (Magic Tree House Fact Tracker)

Texas Revolution by Christopher Forest (Turning Points in U.S. History)

The Texas Revolution by Xina M. Uhl (Expansion of Our Nation)

To the Last Man: The Battle of the Alamo by John Micklos, Jr. (Fact Finders)

What Was the Alamo? by Pam Pollack (Who HQ)

	The Book You Chose	Date Completed
34.1 *Light Reader*		
34.2 *Interested Reader*		
34.3 *Avid Reader*		
34.4 *Committed Reader*		
34.5 *Enthralled Reader*		

Railroads/Trains

Challenge 35

Blind Tom: The Horse Who Helped Build the Great Railroad by Shirley Raye Redmond

The Building of the Transcontinental Railroad by Nathan Olson (Graphic Library)

Building the Transcontinental Railroad by Jessica Rusick (This or That? History Edition)

Building the Transcontinental Railroad: An Interactive Engineering Adventure by Steven Otfinoski (You Choose: Engineering Marvels)

Caboose Mystery by Gertrude Chandler Warner (The Boxcar Children)

Cascade Mountain Railroad Mysteries series by Anne Capeci

Casey Jones by Larry Dane Brimner

Casey Jones by Steven Krensky (On My Own)

Casey Jones by Andrea P. Smith (Jr. Graphic American Legends)

Casey Jones and His Railroad Legacy by Christopher Alber

Children of the Orphan Trains by Holly Littlefield

Connecting the Coasts: The Race to Build the Transcontinental Railroad by Norma Lewis (Fact Finders)

Coolies by Yin

The Fastest Train in the West by Geronimo Stilton

The Great Train Mystery by Carole Marsh (Real Kids, Real Places)

The Happy Hollisters and the Whistle-Pig Mystery by Jerry West

I Escaped Egypt's Deadliest Train Disaster by Scott Peters

I Survived the Wellington Avalanche, 1910 by Lauren Tarshis

It Happened on a Train by Mac Barnett (Brixton Brothers)

Journey on a Runaway Train by Gertrude Chandler Warner (The Boxcar Children)

The Iron Dragon Never Sleeps by Stephen Krensky

Locomotive by Brian Floca

The Midnight Adventure of Kate Shelley, Train Rescuer by Margaret K. Wetterer (History's Kid Heroes)

The Mystery of the Orphan Train by Gertrude Chandler Warner (The Boxcar Children)

The Mystery on the Train by Gertrude Chandler Warner (The Boxcar Children)

Nat Love by Deborah Underwood (History Maker Bios)

Nate the Great on the Owl Express by Marjorie Weinman Sharmat

Orphan Train by Verla Kay

Orphan Trains: An Interactive History Adventure by Elizabeth Raum (You Choose)

The Railway Children by E. Nesbit

See Inside Trains by Emily Bone and Colin King (Usborne)

Strangers on a Train by Carolyn Keene (Nancy Drew Diaries)

Ten Mile Day and the Building of the Transcontinental Railroad by Mary Ann Fraser

Terror on the Train by Terry Deary (Victorian Tales)

Train to Nowhere by Zander Bingham (Jack Jones)

Train to Somewhere by Eve Bunting

Trains! by Susan E. Goodman (Step Into Reading)

The Transcontinental Railroad by John Perritano (A True Book)

Trapped on the D.C. Train! by Ron Roy (Capital Mysteries)

The Twisted Tunnels by Terry Deary (Victorian Tales)

The Vanishing Passenger by Gertrude Chandler Warner (The Boxcar Children)

We Were There at the Driving of the Golden Spike by David Shepherd

You Wouldn't Want to Work on the Railroad! by Ian Graham

	The Book You Chose	Date Completed
35.1 *Light Reader*		
35.2 *Interested Reader*		
35.3 *Avid Reader*		
35.4 *Committed Reader*		
35.5 *Enthralled Reader*		

Gold Rush

Challenge 36

California

By the Great Horn Spoon! by Sid Fleischman

California Gold Rush by Veronica B. Wilkins (Turning Points in U.S. History)

The California Gold Rush: An Interactive History Adventure by Elizabeth Raum (You Choose)

The California Gold Rush and the '49ers by Jean F. Blashfield (Fact Finders)

Gold! Gold from the American River! January 24, 1848: The Day the Gold Rush Began by Don Brown (Actual Times)

Gold Rush! by Jesse Wiley (The Oregon Trail)

The "Gosh Awful" Gold Rush Mystery by Carole Marsh (Real Kids, Real Places)

I Escaped the Gold Rush Fever: A California Gold Rush Survival Story by Scott Peters

If You Were a Kid During the California Gold Rush by Josh Gregory

John Sutter and the California Gold Rush by Matt Doeden (Graphic Library)

Joining the California Gold Rush by Jessica Rusick (This or That? History Edition)

Light a Candle: A Story of Chinese American Pioneers on Gold Mountain by Jean Kuo Lee (I Am America)

Penny by Whitney Sanderson (Horse Diaries)

Sarah Journeys West: An Oregon Trail Survival Story by Nikki Shannon Smith (Girls Survive)

Strike It Rich! The Story of the California Gold Rush by Brianna Hall (Fact Finders)

What Was the Gold Rush? by Joan Holub (Who HQ)

Klondike

Archie Strikes Gold by Brandon Terrell

The Bite of the Gold Bug: A Story of the Alaskan Gold Rush by Barthe DeClements (Once Upon America)

Call of the Klondike by David Meissner and Kim Richardson

Down the Yukon by Will Hobbs

Fire and Snow: A Tale of the Alaskan Gold Rush by J. Gunderson

Gold Rush Fever: A Story of the Klondike, 1898 by Barbara Greenwood

Gold Rush Winter by Claire Rudolf Murphy (Stepping Stones)

Jason's Gold by Will Hobbs

Jasper and the Riddle of Riley's Mine by Caroline Starr Rose

The Klondike by Jean Leturgie (Lucky Luke)

Murphy: Gold Rush Dog by Alison Hart (Dog Chronicles)

We Were There at the Klondike Gold Rush by Benjamin Appel

Other

Hard Gold: The Colorado Gold Rush of 1859 by Avi

Jo's Journey by Nikki Tate (Orca Young Readers)

The Mystery of the Lost Mine by Gertrude Chandler Warner

Zion Gold Rush by C.R. Fulton (The Campground Kids)

	The Book You Chose	**Date Completed**
36.1 *Light Reader*		
36.2 *Interested Reader*		
36.3 *Avid Reader*		
36.4 *Committed Reader*		
36.5 *Enthralled Reader*		

Book Awards & Party

Do This as Soon as You Finish Your Reading Challenge

Grab your child's completed reading log and help him fill out the awards page (opposite page) to give his best and worst books an official award and mark them as most memorable this year.

Encourage him not to agonize over "was this one really the best..." but to go with his general impressions or write down all the contenders.

Send us a copy of this at books@timberdoodle.com, and we'll be thrilled to credit you 50 Doodle Dollar Reward points (worth $2.50 off your next order) as our thank-you for taking the time to share. We'll also congratulate your child on a job so well done!

Bonus Idea

Have an awards ceremony night all about one of the books on your list! You'll get the most specific ideas by searching online for "book I picked theme party," but here are some things to think through as you get started.

Food: How can you tie the menu to the theme? A book like *Green Eggs and Ham* or *Pancakes for Breakfast* is easy—just replicate the food in the book! If you're working with a book that doesn't feature food directly, there are a few options. Perhaps the book featured a construction crew; you could all eat from "lunchboxes" tonight or set up your kitchen to masquerade as a food truck. Or if you're reading a book about the pioneers, do a little research and eat frying pan bread, beans, venison, and cornmeal mush.

You could also take the food you would normally eat and reshape it to match your story. For instance, sandwiches can be cut into ships, round apple slices can be life preservers, crackers can be labeled "hardtack," and you're well on your way to a party featuring your favorite nautical tale.

Don't forget the setting. As ridiculous as it sounds, eating dinner by (battery-operated!) lantern light under your table draped with blankets will make that simple camping tale an experience your family will be recalling for years to come.

Or perhaps some handmade red table fans, softly playing traditional Chinese music, and a red tablecloth would provide the perfect backdrop for the story about life in China.

The more senses you use, the more memorable you make this experience. Use appropriate background music, diffuse peppermint oil to make it smell like Christmas, dim the lights, eat at the top of the swing set, or whatever would set this apart from a regular night and make it just a bit crazy and fun.

Don't get trapped in either the "we must do this tonight" mode or the "we can't do this because it won't be perfect" mode. Allowing your child to spend a few days creating decorations and menus is wonderful! Doing it today because it's the only free night on the horizon even though you can only integrate a few ideas into the preset menu? Also amazing! Your goal is to value the book and make some fun memories.

Book Awards of

_____

(YOUR CHILD'S NAME HERE)   (YEAR HERE)

I READ _____ BOOKS FROM THE READING CHALLENGE THIS YEAR!

FUNNIEST BOOK:
_____

MOST MEMORABLE BOOK:
_____

BOOK I READ THE MOST TIMES:
_____

BOOK I ENJOYED THE LEAST:
_____

TEACHER'S FAVORITE BOOK:
_____

BOOK I MOST WISH WAS A SERIES:
_____

CHOOSE YOUR OWN AWARD:
_____

_____

When You're Done Here

Your Top 4 FAQ about Next Year

Things to Think through as You Anticipate Fourth Grade

So you're finishing up third grade already? How has it gone for you? Really, we'd love to know! (Plus, you get reward points for your review.) Just jump over to the Third-Grade Curriculum page on our website and scroll down to submit a review.

As you look toward next year, there are a few things that you may want to know.

1. When Can We See the New Kits?

New kits usually release in April. Check our Facebook page or give us a call for this year's projection, but it's always in the spring and usually mid-April.

2. Free Customization

If your child has raced ahead in some subjects this year, or if you need to go back and fill in some gaps, or if you don't need more Math-U-See blocks, you'll be thrilled to know that you can customize your kit next year. You'll find full details on our website, but know that customization is free and can often be completed online if you prefer to DIY.

3. Do I Need to Take the Summer Off?

Some students finish a grade with an eager passion to jump right into the next grade, and parents contact us asking if that's OK or if they should take some time off so the child doesn't burn out. We are year-round homeschoolers, so we would definitely be fans of jumping into the next grade!

However, the truth is that this is your decision. We can tell you that a long break can quench the thirst for knowledge, and that's why our family typically moves right into the next grade. However, sometimes a little suspense makes the year begin with beautiful anticipation. If you have a crazy summer planned, it can be ideal to set school aside and enjoy the season!

If you decide to start early, you could consider saving 1 or 2 items for your official start date so that there is still some anticipation.

4. Can I Refill This Kit for My Next Child?

Absolutely! Each year's Additional Student Kit reflects the current year's kit (so the 2024-2025 Elite Curriculum Kit and the 2024-2025 Additional Student Kit correlate). If you loved it just the way it was, refill it now before we swap things around for next year. Or, if you prefer, wait for the new kits to launch and then let our team help you figure out what tweaks (if any) need to be made.

We're Here to Help!

If you have other questions for us, want to share additional feedback, or would like to get in touch for some other reason, don't hesitate to drop us a line or give us a call. (FYI, we also have online chat on our website if that's easier for you.)

mail@Timberdoodle.com
800-478-0672

Doodle Dollar Reward Points

What They Are, How They Work, and Where to Find Them

If you're one of our Charter School BFFs, we just want to give you a heads up that the following information doesn't really apply to you. Doodle Dollars are earned on individual prepaid orders (credit cards or online payment plans are fine) and sadly don't apply to purchase orders or school district orders.

Now, with that out of the way, here's the good news. Almost any item you order directly from us earns you reward points!

You will earn 1 point for every $1 you spend.
20 points = $1 off a future order!

Some families prefer to use this money as they go, while others save it up for Christmas or for those midyear purchases that just weren't in the budget.

Can I Earn More Points?

Absolutely! Review your purchases on Timberdoodle.com to earn points. Add pictures for even more points!

What Can I Spend My Points On?

Anything on our website. These reward points act as a gift certificate to be used on anything you like.

How Do I Get to My Points?

The simplest way is to look for the teal Doodle Dollars pop-up in the lower left corner of our website. Click it, log in, then click "All Rewards" > "Redeem" and drag the slider to choose how many points to cash out. You'll immediately be issued a gift certificate to apply to your order. If you run into any challenges, please let our team know, and we will be thrilled to assist you.

Check our website for the latest information on reward points:
www.Timberdoodle.com/doodledollars

Photo: The Browns in Miami, Florida

Printed in the USA
CPSIA information can be obtained
at www.ICGtesting.com
JSHW050836290824
68904JS00002B/15

9 781958 140628